DREAMLAND'S

GRADED MATHEMATICS

PART - 4

By
SUSHMA NAYAR
M.Sc. I (D.U.), B. Ed.
H.O.D Mathematics
Delhi Public School,
Mathura Road, New Delhi-3

Published by

DREAMLAND PUBLICATIONS

J-128, KIRTI NAGAR, NEW DELHI - 110 015, (INDIA)
Fax : 011-2543 8283 Tel : 011-2510 6050
E-mail : dreamland@vsnl.com
www.dreamlandpublications.com

Published in 2011 by
DREAMLAND PUBLICATIONS
J-128, Kirti Nagar, New Delhi - 110 015 (India)
Tel : 011-2510 6050, Fax : 011-2543 8283
Copyright © 2011 Dreamland Publications
ISBN 81-7301-261-X
Printed at : **Shalini Offset Press**

Preface

Graded Mathematics is a series of nine books—Parts 0 to 8— meant for children of KG to class VIII . The series is a beautiful blend of the text and the pictures. It is a class by itself as far as the subject of Mathematics is concerned.

The topics in each book are in conformity with the latest syllabi issued by the NCERT. They have been pictorially graded in such a manner as to suit the needs of the concerned age-group. The children have been introduced to each topic through pictures so that they may grasp the topic without much difficulty.

There are a host of black-and-white books on Mathematics flooding the market. But the books of our series are off the beaten track. As far as the designing in our books is concerned it is in line with international standards.

We are glad to place this unique series in the hands of the teachers and the taught with the hope that it will admirably meet their approval from every angle. Constructive suggestions for the betterment of the series are highly welcome.

— AUTHOR

Contents

1 WHAT WE HAVE LEARNT

A. Read these numerals and write them in words :

1. 999 _____

2. 9,593 _____

3. 8,565 _____

4. 4,025 _____

5. 50,657 _____

6. 99,999 _____

B. Read these numbers and write them in figures :

1. Seven thousand and seventy. _____

2. Nine thousand and nine. _____

3. Five thousand nine hundred and seven. _____

4. Seven thousand five hundred and forty-two. _____

5. Eighty-four thousand nine hundred and eleven _____

6. Ninety-nine thousand nine hundred and ninety-nine _____

7. Seventy-nine thousand eight hundred and forty. _____

8. Seventy thousand nine hundred and nine. _____

9. Eighty thousand and eighty-nine. _____

C. **Which is the greater ?**

1. 7070 or 7007 ?   2. 9909 or 9999 ?

3. 4735 or 4753 ?   4. 13842 or 13824 ?

5. 46802 or 64802 ?   6. 8889 or 8988 ?

D. **Write**

1. the smallest 2-digit number.

2. the largest 2-digit number.

3. the smallest 3-digit number.

4. the largest 3-digit number.

5. the smallest 4-digit number.

6. the largest 4-digit number.

7. the smallest 5-digit number.

8. the largest 5-digit number.

E. **Fill up the blanks :**

(a) 1. 4,976 = _____ + _____ + 70+ _____

2. 79,792 = 70000 + _____ + _____ + _____ +2

3. 73,642 = _____ +3000 + _____ + _____ + _____

(b) 4. 70000+900+20+4   = _____

5. 30000+6000+800   = _____

6. 60000+7000+300+40+2   = _____

F. **Write in the ascending as well as in the descending orders :**

_____

1. 709, 907, 4321, 3412   _____

_____

2. 27935, 58053, 23085, 58503   _____

_____

3. 26402, 54620, 46204, 84206   _____

G. Write in words :

1. $\frac{5}{6}$ _____   2. $\frac{2}{11}$ _____

3. $\frac{3}{13}$ _____   4. $\frac{1}{8}$ _____

H. Fill up each blank with the correct figure :

1.
```
    5 1 7 6 □ 3
  + 1 4 5 □ 5 4
  ─────────────
  □ □ 3 4 3 □
```

2.
```
      4 □ 5 7
  + 3 □ 0 6 □
  ───────────
  □ 8 2 1 7
```

3.
```
    3 5 3 □ 6
  + □ 3 7 3 □
  ───────────
    7 □ 0 4 5
```

4.
```
    3 □ 4 □ 7
  - 2 0 2 7 □
  ───────────
    1 6 1 8 3
```

5.
```
    8 7 3 □ 5
  - 6 4 □ 3 4
  ───────────
    2 3 2 8 1
```

6.
```
    3 2 □ 4 2
  -   9 1 4 □
  ───────────
    2 3 3 9 3
```

7.
```
        □ 5 9
    x   1 2 3
    ─────────
        4 7 7
      3 □ 8 x
    1 □ 9 x x
    ─────────
    1 9 5 5 7
```

8.
```
  31 ) 7 1 9 3 ( 2 3 □
       - 6 2
       ───────
         9 9
       - □ 3
       ───────
           6 3
         - 6 □
         ───────
             1
```

I. Which is the greater :

(a) $\frac{5}{8}$ or $\frac{9}{16}$?   (b) $\frac{2}{9}$ or $\frac{7}{36}$?

(c) $\frac{4}{5}$ or $\frac{19}{25}$?   (d) $\frac{7}{11}$ or $\frac{29}{36}$?

J. Find the value of :

(a) 36 x 178 + 64 x 178

(b) 7 x 4599 + 3 x 4599

(c) $\frac{5}{8} + \frac{2}{8} - \frac{7}{8}$

6

K. **Write the time in a.m. or p.m.**

(a) 5:30 in the evening **5:30 p.m.**

(b) 11:05 in the morning

(c) 3:30 in the morning

(d) 7:15 in the evening

(e) 1:35 in the afternoon

(f) 9:50 in the night

L. **What time will it be after 5 hours ?**

(a) 4:35 a.m. **9:35 a.m.**

(b) 11:00 p.m.

(c) 2:45 a.m.

(d) 12 noon

(e) 12 mid-night

(f) 6:50 a.m.

M. **What time was it before 3 hours ?**

(a) 8:40 p.m. 5:40 p.m.

(b) 5:40 a.m.

(c) 12 noon

(d) 12 mid-night

(e) 7:30 p.m.

(f) 4:05 a.m.

N. **Fill up each blank, using a.m. or p.m.**

(a) The sun rises at 5:59 ———

(b) My sister goes to bed at 10:30 ———

(c) I go to play at 4:00 ———

(d) I go to school at 7:00 ———

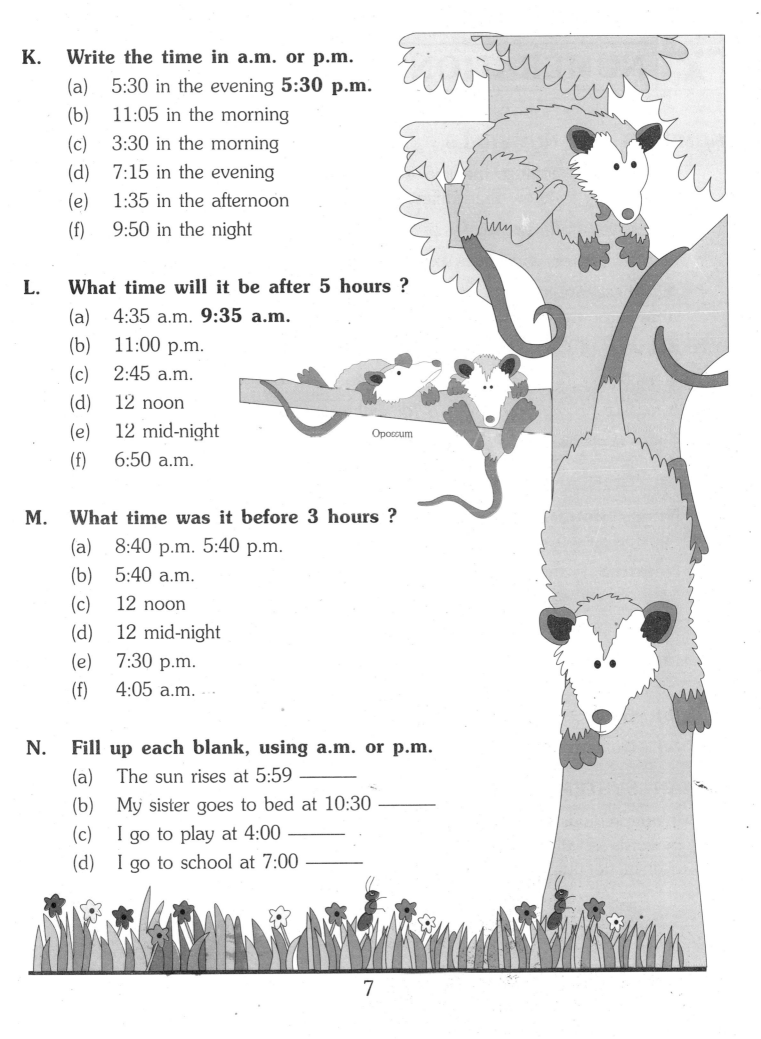

Opossum

2 NUMERATION AND NOTATION

(INDIAN SYSTEM)

NUMBERS AND NUMERALS

We generally confuse the two words—*number* and *numeral.* So, it is desirable to know their difference.

When we count, we say —

one, *two, three, four, five, six, seven, eight,* nine .... etc.

All these are *names* of numbers. So, they are called **number-names** or **numbers.**

But each of these numbers is written through a *symbol* also ; e.g.

1 for one   2 for two   3 for *three*   4 for four   5 *for five*

6 fox six   7 *for seven*   8 *for eight*   9 *for nine*

These symbols 1,2,3,4,5,6,7,8,9 are called numerals.

NUMERATION AND NOTATION

Numeration *is the process of expressing a numeral in words; as—* one for 1, two for 2, three for 3 etc.

Notation is the *process of representing number-names by their symbols, i.e. expressing them in numerals (figures).*

So, it is clear that —

(a) *Number* is a common word used for any count in words or figures.

(b) *Number-name* is the expression of a count in words.

(c) *Numeral* is the expression of a count in figures.

INDIAN SYSTEM OF NUMBERS

In our previous class, we learnt to count and write numbers up to 99999 in words as well as in figures. Here in this chapter, we shall learn about even higher numbers.

We know that —

(a)   One more than nine is ten $(9+1=\mathbf{10})$.

(b)   One more than ninety-nine is hundred $(99+1=\mathbf{100})$.

(c)   One more than nine hundred and ninety-nine is a thousand $(999+1=\mathbf{1000})$.

(d)   One more than nine thousand nine hundred and ninety-nine is ten thousand $(9999+1=\mathbf{10000})$.

(e)   One more than ninety-nine thousand nine hundred and ninety-nine is one lakh $(99999+1=\mathbf{100000})$.

It is clear that —

The numeral 100000 is called **one lakh** in the Indian System of counting. It is the smallest 6-digit number. It is equal to 100 thousands.

Numbers Beyond One Lakh

We extend the numbers beyond one lakh in the same way as we do from one to one lakh.

One lakh	100000
Two lakh	200000
Three lakh	300000
------------	---------
------------	---------
------------	---------
------------	---------
------------	---------
Nine lakh	900000

9

Now we read —

532251 as Five lakh thirty-two thousand two hundred and fifty-one.

999999 as Nine lakh ninety-nine thousand nine hundred and ninety-nine.

999999 is the largest 6-digit number.

1 more than 999999 is **1000000.**

We read 1000000 as ten lakh.

1000000 is the smallest 7-digit number.

9999999 in the largest 7-digit number.

1 more than 9999999 is **10000000**

We read 10000000 as one crore.

10000000 is the smallest 8-digit number.

Lakhs		Thousands		Units		
Ten Lakhs	Lakhs	Ten Thousands	Thousands	Hundreds	Tens	units
1	0	0	0	0	0	0

Exercise

I. Write as numerals :

   a. Twenty-eight lakh sixty-seven thousand five hundred and thirty-seven.

   b. Fifty-seven lakh seventy-five thousand eight hundred and nineteen.

   c. Three lakh eight thousand seven hundred and forty-three.

   d. Twenty-five lakh one thousand seven hundred and forty-nine.

   e. Nine lakh nine thousand and nine.

II. Write in the ascending order :

   f. 3850784, 3100308, 3874643, 5103731

   g. 8673742, 4345471, 9999999, 4037009

   h. 4251576, 7825482, 4013821, 3507286

III. Write in the descending order :

   i. 3000004, 3237503, 3426871, 4000003

   j. 4545445, 4546445, 4545545, 4545554

   k. 6336363, 3663363, 3663636, 3636366

IV. Write two more terms in each series :

   l. 6616632, 6626632, 6636632, ———— , ————

   m. 5253511, 6243511, 7233611, ———— , ————

V. Numerate the following numbers :

   n. 399045   **o.** 575908   **p.** 583089

   q. 4897205   **r.** 9904050   **s.** 7890892

   t. 8307985   **u.** 8593073   **v.** 7920114

   w. 8792013   **x.** 3079652

3 EXPANDED FORM AND PLACE VALUE

A. Expanded form

We get the expanded form of a numeral by spreading it out in full. Let us take an example to grasp this fact properly.

The number 7,45,368 will be read as —

Seven lakh forty-five thousand three hundred and sixty-eight.

Now —

(a)   Seven lakh = 7,00,000

(b)   Forty-five thousand = 45,000 = 40,000 + 5,000

(c)   Three hundred = 300

(d)   Sixty-eight = 68 = 60 + 8

So, the expanded form of
7,45,368 = 7,00,000 + 40,000 + 5,000 + 300 + 60 + 8

Similarly, 99,99,999 when expanded will be
= 90,00,000 + 9,00,000 + 90,000 + 9,000 + 900 + 90 + 9

White Chester Belly Squirrel

B. Place value
Introduction to place value of a 6-digit number

The **8** stands for 8 lakhs   8,00, 000

The **3** stands for 3 ten thousands   + 30,000

The **6** stands for 6 thousands   +   6,000

The **0** stands for 0 hundreds

The **4** stands for 4 tens or forty   +   40

The **7** stands for 7 units   +   7

So, eight lakh thirty-six thousand

and forty-seven is written as   8,36,047

Units	Units	7
	Tens	4
	Hundreds	0
Thousands	Thousands	6
	Ten Thousands	3
Lakhs	Lakhs	8

Oral Work

Read the number. Then tell how many lakhs, ten thousands, thousands, hundreds, tens and units there are in each of the following numbers.

1. (a) 365047 (b) 451367 (c) 526003
2. (a) 402653 (b) 247198 (c) 470520
3. (a) 740298 (b) 532724 (c) 326070
4. (a) 635081 (b) 645367 (c) 400035
5. (a) 724506 (b) 824359 (c) 420500
6. (a) 813290 (c) 913272 (c) 803209

Complete the following.

7. 346281 means —— lakhs, —— ten thousands, —— thousands, —— hundreds, —— tens and —— units

8. 524360 means —— lakhs, —— ten thousands, —— thousands, —— hundreds, —— tens and —— units

9. 206472 means —— lakhs, —— ten thousands, —— thousands, —— hundreds, —— tens and —— units

10. 560329 means —— lakhs, —— ten thousands, —— thousands, —— hundreds, —— tens and —— units

11. 632048 means —— lakhs, —— ten thousands, —— thousands, —— hundreds, —— tens and —— units

12. **How many thousands are there in :**

    (a) 200000 ?   (b) 300000 ?   (c) 450000 ?   (d) 710000 ?

    (e) 423000 ?   (f) 503000 ?   (g) 247000 ?   (h) 560000 ?

13. **How many hundreds are there in :**

    (a) 300000 ?   (b) 400000 ?   (c) 560000 ?   (d) 527000 ?

    (e) 632400 ?   (f) 530700 ?   (g) 689300 ?   (h) 271400 ?

14. Complete the following.

(a) 2 lakhs, 3 ten thousands, 5 thousands, 6 hundreds, 8 tens and 6 units is _____.

(b) 5 lakhs, 6 ten thousands, 0 thousands, 4 hundreds, 9 tens and 4 units is _____.

(c) 3 lakhs, 4 ten thousands, 5 thousands, 0 hundreds, 5 tens and 8 units is _____.

(d) 6 lakhs, 7 ten thousands, 3 thousands, 2 hundreds, 0 tens and 5 units is _____.

C. Look at this :

In 217052—The 7 stands for 7 thousands   (7,000)

In 712520—The 7 stands for 7 lakhs   (7,00,000)

In 172205—The 7 stands for 7 ten thousands   (70,000)

In 502721—The 7 stands for 7 hundreds   (700)

In 250271—The 7 stands for 7 tens   (70)

In 210527—The 7 stands for 7 units   (7)

What does the coloured digit in each numeral stand for ?

15.	(a) 327000	(b) 372000	(c) 732000
16.	(a) 453264	(b) 453624	(c) 453246
17.	(a) 479232	(b) 947232	(c) 794232
18.	(a) 792473	(b) 291374	(c) 910732
19.	(a) 316402	(b) 306412	(c) 364021

D. Look at this :

3,33,333 =   3,00,000
              +30,000
              + 3,000
              +   300
              +   30
              +   3

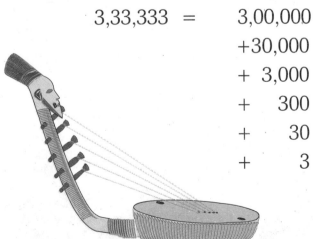

Complete the following.

20. $4,44,444 = 4,00,000+40,000+4,000+$ _____ $+40+4$

21. $7,77,777 = 7,00,000+70,000+7,000+700+$ ___ $+7$

22. $3,26,418 =$ _____ $+20,000+6,000+400+10+8$

E. Building up 6-digit numbers

Look at this :

$7,00,000+30,000+2,000+400+10+6 \quad = 7,32,416$

$7,00,000+30,000+2,000+400+10 \qquad = 7,32,410$

$7,00000+30,000+2,000+400+ \ 6 \qquad = 7,32,406$

$7,00,000+30,000+2,000+10+ \ 6 \qquad = 7,32,016$

$7,00,000+30,000+ \ 400+10+ \ 6 \qquad = 7,30,416$

$7,00,000+2,000+400+10+ \ 6 \qquad = 7,02,416$

Find the value of the following.

23. $1,00,000+10,000+1,000+100+10$

24. $1,00,000+10,000+1,000+100+1$

25. $1,00,000+10,000+1,000+10+1$

26. $1,00,000+1,000+100+10+1$

27. $10,000+1,000+100+10+1$

F. Breaking down 6-digit numbers

Look at this :

$1,11,111 = 1,00,000+10,000+1,000+100+10+1$

$1,01,111 = 1,00,000+1,000+100+10+1$

$1,11,011 = 1,00,000+10,000+1,000+10+1$

$1,10,I11 = 1,00,000+10,000+100+10+1$

$1,11,101 = 1,00,000+10,000+1,000+100+1$

$1,11,110 = 1,00,000+10,000+1,000+100+10$

Fer-de-lance

15

Greater Fruit Bat

G. **Break down the following 6-digit numbers into lakhs, ten thousands, thousands, hundreds, tens and units.**

28. (a) 124673   (b) 471236   (c) 714632
29. (a) 222022   (b) 202222   (c) 220222
30. (a) 222202   (b) 222220   (c) 222222
31. (a) 300871   (b) 352001   (c) 350071
32. (a) 400091   (b) 466001   (c) 462006

H. **Introduction to place value of a 7-digit number**

Lakhs		Thousands		Units		
Ten Lakhs	Lakhs	Ten Thousands	Thousands	Hundreds	Tens	Units
9	8	3	6	0	4	7

The **9** stands for 9 ten lakhs   90,00,000

The **8** stands for 8 lakhs   8,00, 000

The **3** stands for 3 ten thousands   30,000

The **6** stands for 6 thousands   6,000

The **0** stands for 0 hundreds

The **4** stands for 4 tens or forty   40

The **7** stands for 7 units   7

So, ninety-eight lakh thirty-six thousand and forty-seven is written as   98,36,047

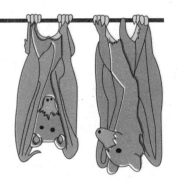

I. Renaming numbers
Look at this :

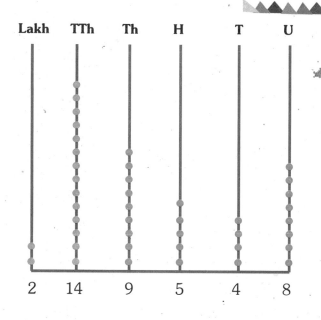

Lakh	TTh	Th	H	T	U
2	14	9	5	4	8

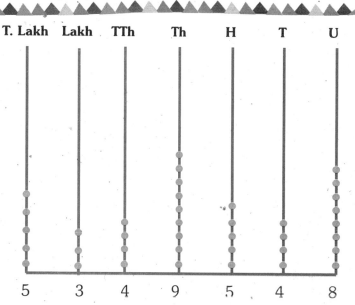

T. Lakh	Lakh	TTh	Th	H	T	U
5	3	4	9	5	4	8

2 lakhs,

14 ten thousands,

9 thousands,

5 hundreds,

4 tens and 8 units

5 ten lakhs,

3 lakhs,

4 ten thousands,

9 thousands,

5 hundreds,

4 tens and 8 units

Write the numeral that means :

33. 4 lakhs, 12 ten thousands, 8 thousands, 4 hundreds, 6 tens and 9 units

34. 6 ten lakhs, 3 lakhs, 6 ten thousands, 11 thousands, 2 hundreds, 5 tens and 8 units

35. 5 ten lakhs, 2 lakhs, 4 ten thousands, 3 thousands, 15 hundreds, 6 tens and 9 units

36. 8 ten lakhs, 1 lakh, 0 ten thousands, 2 thousands, 4 hundreds, 13 tens and 5 units

37. 2 ten lakhs, 5 lakhs, 2 ten thousands, 0 thousands, 5 hundreds, 7 tens and 12 units

Look at this :

29,320   =   2 ten thousands + 9 thousands + 3 hundreds + 2 tens + 0 units

               =   2 ten thousands + 9 thousands + 3 hundreds + 1 ten + 10 units

               =   2 ten thousands + 9 thousands + 2 hundreds + 11 tens + 10 units

               =   2 ten thousands + 8 thousands + 12 hundreds + 11 tens + 10 units

Complete the following.

38.   3,24,562   =   3 lakhs + 2 ten thousands + 4 thousands + 5 hundreds + 6 tens + 2 units

                 =   3 lakhs + 2 ten thousands + 4 thousands + 5 hundreds + 5 tens + __ units

                 =   3 lakhs + 2 ten thousands + 4 thousands + 4 hundreds + __ tens + 12 units

                 =   3 lakhs + 2 ten thousands + 3 thousands + __ hundreds + 15 tens + 12 units

                 =   3 lakhs + 1 ten thousand + __ thousands + 14 hundreds + 15 tens + 12 units

                 =   2 lakhs + 12 ten thousands + 2 thousands + __ hundreds + 6 tens + 2 units

39.   53,17,285   =   5 ten lakhs + 3 lakhs + 1 ten thousand + 7 thousands + 2 hundreds + 8 tens + 5 units

                 =   5 ten lakhs + 3 lakhs + 1 ten thousand + 7 thousands + 2 hundreds + 7 tens + __ units

                 =   5 ten lakhs + 3 lakhs + 1 ten thousand + 7 thousands + 1 hundred + __ tens + 15 units

                 =   5 ten lakhs + 3 lakhs + 1 ten thousand + 6 thousands + __ hundreds + 17 tens + 15 units

                 =   5 ten lakhs + 3 lakhs + 0 ten thousands + — thousands + 11 hundreds + 17 tens + 15 units

                 =   5 ten lakhs + 2 lakhs + __ ten thousands + 16 thousands + 11 hundreds + 17 tens + 15 units

                 =   4 ten lakhs + 9 lakhs + 40 ten thousands + __ thousands + 2 hundreds + 8 tens + 5 units

J. **From each pair of numbers, choose the larger.**

  (a) 382049   (b) 2425361 (c) 3217487

      832049   2452361   3214787

  (d) 316273   (e) 300524   (f) 6508924

      316723   300514   6508928

Collared Lizard

K. **From each pair of numbers, choose the smaller.**

  (a) 213456   (b) 2374298 (c) 405612

      321456   5324798   406512

  (d) 7123456 (e) 342798   (f) 2401562

      6729468   381425   1259406

  (g) 3729648 (h) 1813425 (i) 205946

      2729486   5483125   295046

L. **Rearrange the numbers in each set from the smallest to the largest.**

  (a) 343529   5243529   2443529   543529

  (b) 2362850   382850   5372850   392850

  (c) 1367825   368825   3362825   365825

  (d) 2453746   453246   453646   4453446

  (e) 5428107   8421107   428207   421207

  (f) 1234627   2234617   234527   234517

  (g) 3428536   428566   9428576   428586

  (h) 2361493   6361498   361492   361494

  (i) 2208952   270952   278052   9278902

  (j) 1300572   5304502   364002   364500

4 ADDITION AND SUBTRACTION

A.   Addition of 6 - and 7 - digit numbers without carrying

Look at these :

(1)   2,34,057 + 3,22,242

$$\begin{array}{r} 2,34,057 \\ + 3,22,242 \\ \hline 5,56,299 \\ \hline \end{array}$$

(2)   21,34,276 + 56,52,103

$$\begin{array}{r} 21,34,276 \\ + 56,52,103 \\ \hline 77,86,379 \\ \hline \end{array}$$

Do these in the same way.

1.   (a)   1342472   (b) 1327524   (c)   345235   (d)   234567
      +1432513   +3151415   +214423   +654321

2.   (a)   2463585   (b)   305262   (c)   325634   (d) 2461021
      +4331412   +402035   + 433232   +2026428

3.   (a)   2243512   (b)   234722   (c)   432425   (d) 1357915
      + 5304267   + 561175   + 253512   +1312034

4.   (a)   4010261   (b)   405802   (c)   405032   (d) 1234565
      +3272638   +301104   +240350   +6543214

B. Addition of 6-digit numbers with carrying
Look at this :

$$214235 + 316368$$

Step 1 Adding units	Step 2 Adding tens	Step 3 Adding hundreds
2 1 4 2 3 5 3 1 6 3 6 8 ——————— 3	2 1 4 2 3 5 3 1 6 3 6 8 ——————— 0 3	1 1 4 2 3 5 3 1 6 3 6 8 ——————— 6 0 3
5+8 = 13	1+3+6 = 10	1+2+3 = 6

Step 4 Adding thousands	Step 5 Adding ten thousands	Step 6 Adding lakhs
1 1 1 2 1 4 2 3 5 1 1 6 3 6 8 ——————— 0 6 0 3	1 1 1 3 1 4 2 3 5 4 1 6 3 6 8 ——————— 3 0 6 0 3	1 1 1 3 1 4 2 3 5 4 1 6 3 6 8 ——————— 7 3 0 6 0 3
4+6 = 10	1+1+1 = 3	3+4 = 7

Do these in the same way.

1.   (a)   124365
     +232228

    (b)   736382
     + 842235

    (c)   124823
     +235766

    (d)   229382
     +314312

2.   (a)   235426
     +336220

    (b)   947852
     +230925

    (c)   750274
     +540374

    (d)   835027
     +940536

3.   (a)   533246
     +624375

    (b)   345465
     +321717

    (c)   132587
     + 214642

    (d)   448672
     +239273

C. Addition of 7-digit numbers with carrying

Look at this :   4236547 + 5357105

Step 1 Adding Unit	Step 2 Adding tens	Step 3 Adding hundreds

      1
2 3 6 5 4 7
3 5 7 1 0 5
──────────
         2
	
	      1
	2 3 6 5 4 7
	3 5 7 1 0 5
	──────────
	       5 2
		
		      1
		2 3 6 5 4 7
		3 5 7 1 0 5
		──────────
		     6 5 2

7+5=12	1+4+0=5	5+1=6

Step 4 Adding thousands	Step 5 Adding ten thousands	Step 6 Adding lakhs	Step 7 Adding ten lakhs
  1 1 2 3 6 5 4 7 3 5 7 1 0 5 ────────── 3 6 5 2	 1 1 4 2 3 6 5 4 7 5 3 5 7 1 0 5 ────────── 9 3 6 5 2	 1 1 4 2 3 6 5 4 7 5 3 5 7 1 0 5 ────────── 5 9 3 6 5 2	 1 1 4 2 3 6 5 4 7 5 3 5 7 1 0 5 ────────── 9 5 9 3 6 5 2
6 + 7 = 13	1 + 3 + 5 = 9	2 + 3 = 5	4 + 5 = 9

Do these in the same way.

1. (a)   1356582
    + 2423299

  (b)   2357468
     +3341726

  (c)   4264312
     +2428549

  (d)   2195635
     +3424366

2. (a)   2532658
    +4733204

  (b)   3293409
     +3434202

  (c)   4327256
     +4656035

  (d)   1243934
     +132409

3. (a)   2416682
    +3252639

  (b)   2525861
     +4369419

  (c)   4242378
     +4538173

  (d)   3823193
     +2725788

D. **Subtraction of 6- and 7- digit numbers without carrying**

Look at these :

(1) 9,35,897—6,21,452   **(2)** 57,86,845—25,54,623

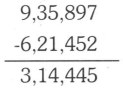

```
    9,35,897                    57,86,245
   -6,21,452                   -25,54,623
   ─────────                   ──────────
    3,14,445                    32,32,222
   ─────────                   ──────────
```

Do these in the same way.

1. (a) 243742   (b) 4876578   (c) 396438   (d) 5376498
    - 122631   -3243225   -164332   -4254362
    ─────────   ─────────   ─────────   ─────────

2. (a) 259369   (b) 5965380   (c) 653794   (d) 7683692
    -124125   -3442160   -221380   -5371231
    ─────────   ─────────   ─────────   ─────────

3. (a) 987765   (b) 8768429   (c) 432493   (d) 7647895
    -726643   -3537119   -321250   -5605043
    ─────────   ─────────   ─────────   ─────────

4. (a) 674468   (b) 7865432   (c) 784368   (d) 6547962
    -543234   -5033211   -673143   -3324851
    ─────────   ─────────   ─────────   ─────────

5. (a) 598796   (b) 9789425   (c) 965674   (d) 8575972
    -287485   -7536012   -123434   -7363401
    ─────────   ─────────   ─────────   ─────────

Turtle
X-ing

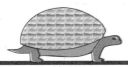
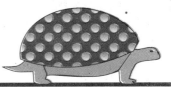

E. Subtraction of 6-digit numbers with carrying

Look at this : 536487 — 224879

Step 1 Subtracting units	Step 2 Subtracting tens	Step 3 Subtracting hundreds
5 3 6 4 ⁷8̷¹7 - 2 2 4 8 7 9 ————— 8	5 3 6 4 ⁷8̷¹7 - 2 2 4 8 7 9 ————— 0 8	5 3⁵6̷¹4⁷8̷¹7 - 2 2 4 8 7 9 ————— 6 0 8
17 — 9 = 8	7 — 7 = 0	14 — 8 = 6

Step 4 Subtracting thousands	Step 5 Subtracting ten thousands	Step 6 Subtracting lakhs
5 3⁵6̷¹4⁷8̷¹7 - 2 2 4 8 7 9 ————— 1 6 0 8	5 3⁵6̷¹4⁷8̷¹7 - 2 2 4 8 7 9 ————— 1 1 6 0 8	5 3⁵6̷¹4⁷8̷¹7 - 2 2 4 8 7 9 ————— 3 1 1 6 0 8
5 — 4 = 1	3 — 2 = 1	5 - 2 = 3

Do these in the same way.

1. (a) 928782
        -644654
        ————

    (b) 245835
        -112681
        ————

    (c) 923543
        -543821
        ————

    (d) 634639
        -525427
        ————

2. (a) 834589
        -596021
        ————

    (b) 235785
        -122942
        ————

    (c) 249345
        -157263
        ————

    (d) 756734
        -325605
        ————

3. (a) 253431
        -121257
        ————

    (b) 685345
        -463629
        ————

    (c) 924343
        -414672
        ————

    (d) 824368
        -615275
        ————

F. Subtraction of 7-digit numbers with carrying

Look at this :   5278462 - 3195674

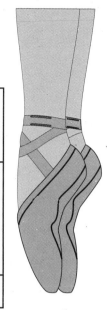

Step 1 Subtracting units	Step 2 Subtracting tens	Step 3 Subtracting hundreds
5 2 7 8 4 ⁵6̸ ¹2 - 3 1 9 5 6 7 4 ———————— 8	5 2 7 8 ³4̸ ¹⁵6̸ ¹2 - 3 1 9 5 6 7 4 ———————— 8 8	5 2 7 ⁷8̸ ¹³4̸ ¹⁵6̸ ¹2 - 3 1 9 5 6 7 4 ———————— 7 8 8
12 - 4 = 8	15 - 7 = 8	13 - 6 = 7

Step 4 Subtracting thousands	Step 5 Subtracting ten thousands	Step 6 Subtracting hundred thousands	Step 7 Subtracting lakhs
5 2 7 ⁷8̸ ¹³4̸ ¹⁵6̸ ¹2 - 3 1 9 5 6 7 4 ———————— 2 7 8 8	5 ¹2 ⁷7 ¹³8̸ ¹⁵4̸ ¹6̸ 2 - 3 1 9 5 6 7 4 ———————— 8 2 7 8 8	5 ¹2 ¹7 ⁷8̸ ¹³4̸ ¹⁵6̸ ¹2 - 3 1 9 5 6 7 4 ———————— 0 8 2 7 8 8	5 ¹2 ¹7 ⁷8̸ ¹³4̸ ¹⁵6̸ ¹2 - 3 1 9 5 6 7 4 ———————— 2 0 8 8 7 2 8
7 — 5 = 2	17 — 9 = 8	1 — 1 = 0	5 - 3 = 2

Do these in the same way.

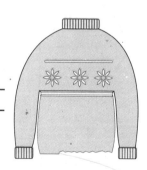

1. (a) 8256784   (b) 3346538   (c) 9256463   (d) 8372489
       -5103026   -2220270   -6104521   -1215377

2. (a) 7348256   (b) 6782986   (c) 4435268   (d) 3253468
       -2153140   -2653774   -2200351   -1142383

3. (a) 5253346   (b) 9875005   (c) 7873287   (d) 2257652
       -3132097   -2643247   -5546943   -1178030

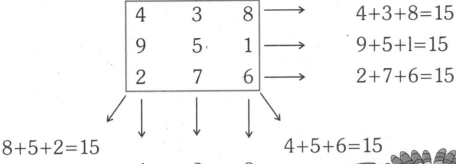

4	3	8	→	4+3+8=15
9	5	1	→	9+5+1=15
2	7	6	→	2+7+6=15

8+5+2=15   4+5+6=15

```
  4     3     8
 +9    +5    +1
 +2    +7    +6
 ──    ──    ──
 15    15    15
```

This is a **magic square.** It has 3 rows and 3 columns. Each little square that contains a number is called a **cell.** The numbers in the cells add vertically, horizontally and diagonally to give the same total. In the example, the magic number (total) is 15.

Complete the following magic squares by filling in the correct numbers in the empty cells. The magic number is written beside each square.

(a)

15		
	20	
5		

60

(b)

4		16
	13	

39

(c)

	95	
		5
50	35	

195

(d)

	6	
78		30
		42

162

H. Puzzles involving addition and subtraction

1. **Complete the addition puzzles.**

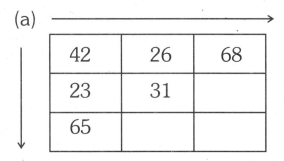

(a)

→		
42	26	68
23	31	
65		

(b)

→		
204	115	
322	233	

2. **Complete the addition puzzles.**

(a)

→		
79	31	48
40	4	
39		

(b)

→		
357	120	
110	100	

3. **For each box give the pair of numbers whose sum and difference are given.**

Sum			Difference
15	**9 + 6**	**9 — 6**	**3**
7			3
9			9
12			4
18			0
20			2
25			19
27			17

I. Further exercises on addition and subtraction

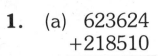

1. (a) 623624   (b) 3487229   (c) 2536725   (d) 3623816
    +218510   +2078418   +1245919   +2610425

2. (a) 473851   (b) 376722   (c) 4523567   (d) 2373825
    +528475   +487635   +2747929   +5943519

3. (a) 3049325   (b) 264932   (c) 3406759   (d) 3492636
    +4064798   +598906   +2807729   +5930836

4. (a) 482465   (b) 728567   (c) 3637825   (d) 4768228
    +519876   +634768   +7437819   +8668315

5. (a) 232312   (b) 3256529   (c) 4285426   (d) 3467459
    -115790   -2444794   -3149756   -2786818

6. (a) 433752   (b) 534333   (c) 3568257   (d) 8364526
    -256805   -360680   -2795425   -45 93716

7. (a) 846520   (b) 7234356   (c) 532025   (d) 924345
    -657984   -5865485   -234756   -567765

8. (a) 430502   (b) 8530028   (c) 7480026   (d) 504022
    -264275   -3724826   -2794518   -457835

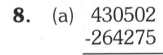

9. (a) 200002   (b) 8300000   (c) 340000   (d) 2500000
    -193467   -2865982   -256345   -1888376

10. (a) 2434961
+1724075

(b) 3623202
+2519054

(c) 1264731
+2284536

(d) 1234842
+3452705

11. (a) 3451233
+3339876

(b) 2399754
+4279345

(c) 2856512
+1569381

(d) 2932545
+3439816

12. (a) 2535087
+2905044

(b) 2925871
+3404956

(c) 378925
+466900

(d) 482760
+482794

13. (a) 259678
+345745

(b) 498776
+326892

(c) 372856
+234779

(d) 299854
+526283

14. (a) 246628
+774503

(b) 356769
+592565

(c) 3646761
+4960855

(d) 235867
+436344

15. (a) 352400
-213689

(b) 3000049
-1256926

(c) 300050
-242321

(d) 7004002
-3562481

16. (a) 7000045
-2413524

(b) 804000
-516247

(c) 5002008
-2361586

(d) 300080
-247532

17. (a) 3524352
-2687461

(b) 434231
-168456

(c) 3013429
-2454568

(d) 502345
-434456

18. (a) 2351436
-1472761

(b) 512324
-245467

(c) 2112227
-1345672

(d) 543232
-367546

5 | MULTIPLICATION & DIVISION

A — MULTIPLICATION

In class III we learnt how to multiply two numbers, the product of which did not exceed 99,999. Now we shall learn how to multiply two numbers, the product of which does not exceed 99,99,999.

Example 1.   Multiply 62879 by 111.

Solution :   *Steps :*

```
      6 2 8 7 9
    x     1 1 1
    _____
      6 2 8 7 9
    6 2 8 7 9 x
  6 2 8 7 9 x x
  _____
  6 9 7 9 5 6 9
```

1.   Multiply by 1 and write the product from under the one's place.

2.   Multiply by 1 and write the product form under the ten's place.

3.   Multiply by 1 and write the product from under the hundred's place.

4.   Add up to get the product.

∴   product = **6979569 Ans.**

Example 2.   Multiply 64564 by 25.

```
        6 4 5 6 4
      x       2 5
      _____
      3 2 2 8 2 0
    1 2 9 1 2 8 x
    _____
    1 6 1 4 1 0 0
```

Solution : *Steps :*

1.   Multiply by 5 and write the product from under the unit's place.

2.   Multiply by 2 and write the product from under the ten's place.

3.   Add up to get the product.

∴   product = **1614100 Ans.**

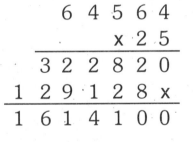

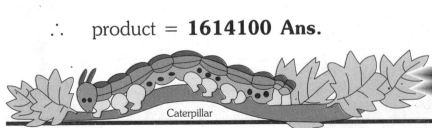

Caterpillar

Example 3. If a cycle factory produces 725 cycles daily, how many cycles will it produce in 287 days ?

Solution : It is clear from the expression that the required number of cycles = 725 x 287.

So, we shall multiply them.

```
      7 2 5
    x 2 8 7
    ─────────
    5 0 7 5
  5 8 0 0 x
1 4 5 0 x x
─────────────
2 0 8 0 7 5
```

∴ required number of cycles = **208075 Ans.**

EXERCISE

I. Find the product :

1. 34421x41	**2.** 43455x51	**3.** 25689x111
4. 45312x44	**5.** 23040x103	**6.** 64361x106
7. 3040x333	**8.** 10503x35	**9.** 4164x60
10. 4310x41	**11.** 4350x120	**12.** 3011x163

II. Find the product :

13. 42904x42	**14.** 75865x45	**15.** 78316x45
16. 6453x78	**17.** 5097x98	**18.** 7019x63
19. 94207x94	**20.** 89355x43	**21.** 7476x84
22. 6765x18	**23.** 3716x386	**24.** 47853x57
25. 98705x29	**26.** 6337x72	**27.** 78755x53

28. 576353x2   29. 434275x3   30. 788154x8

31. 719047x6   32. 310576x3   33. 819532x9

34. 791709x4   35. 519187x9   36. 709836x7

37. The weight of a cotton-bale is 75628 kg. Find the total weight of 65 bales.

38. A baby tricycle costs Rs. 616. Find the total cost of 4346 tricycles.

39. If a transistor costs Rs. 251, find the cost of 30030 transistors.

40. A railway engine can run at a speed of 20809 metres an hour. During a month it worked for 318 hours. How much distance did it cover in all ?

41. A VCR costs Rs. 13447. Find the total cost of 303 VCRs.

42. Multiply 361 and 78 and multiply their product by 67 again.

43. A truck is carrying 7687 packets of biscuits. If a packet contains 635 biscuits, find the total number of biscuits in the truck.

44. A farmer produced 5638 quintals of wheat. He sold it to the FCI at Rs. 173 a quintal. How much money did he get for his wheat ?

45. Write the correct digit for each square.

(a)
```
      4 5 6 7
    x   2 4 9
    ───────────
      4 1 1 0 □
    1 8 □ 6 8 x
    □ 1 3 4 x x
    ───────────
  1 1 □ 7 1 8 3
```

(b)
```
      4 9 3 8
      x   2 5
    ───────────
    2 4 □ 9 0
    □ 8 7 6 x
    ───────────
  1 2 3 4 5 0
```

46. Solve :
(a) 1875x181+1875x182
(b) 1545x609+1114x609+1641x609
(c) 1315x709+1523x709—1138x709

B — DIVISION

In class III, we learnt how to divide a 5-digit number by a 2-digit number. Now we shall learn how to divide a 6-digit or 7-digit number by a 2-digit or 3-digit number.

Before solving some examples on the process of division, we must bear the following facts in mind :

1. The number which is divided is called the **dividend.**
2. The number by which the dividend is divided is the **divisor.**
3. The number that we get as a result of the process of division is called the **quotient.**
4. The number that is left over in the end out of the dividend is called the **remainder.**

Example : Divide 9088456 by 22.

Solution : Steps —

1. We do not know the multiplication table of 22. So, we will use the table of 2, the extreme-left digit of the divisor.
2. Dividend has 9 on its extreme left. We know that 2 x 4 = 8. So, we put 4 in the quotient and write 22 x 4 = 88 under 90 and subtract.
3. Getting 2 as remainder, we bring down 8 from the dividend and get 28.
4. 22 goes into 28 only **1 time.** So, we write 1 in the quotient and write 22 under 28 and subtract to get 6 as remainder.
5. Bringing down 8, we get 68. Now 2 of the divisor goes into 6 of 68 **3 times.** So, 3 is written in the quotient and 3 x 22=66 under 68.
6. Bringing down 4, we get 24. 22 goes into 24 only **1 time.** So, we write 1 in the quotient and write 22 under 24 and subtract to get 2 as reminder.
7. Bringing down 6, we get 25. 22 goes into 25 only **1 time.** So, we write 1 in the quotient and write 22 under 25 and subtract to get 3 as remainder.
8. Bringing down 6, we get 36. 22 goes into 36 only **1 time.** So, we write 1 in the quotient and write 22 under 36 and subtract to get 14 as remainder.

$\therefore$ **quotient = 413111** and **remainder = 14**

```
          4 1 3 1 1 1
   2 2 ) 9 0 8 8 4 5 6
        - 8 8
        ─────
          2 8
        - 2 2
        ─────
          6 8
        - 6 6
        ─────
          2 4
        - 2 2
        ─────
          2 5
        - 2 2
        ─────
          3 6
        - 2 2
        ─────
          1 4
```

EXERCISE

A. **Divide to find the quotient and the reminder :**
1. 569888 by 24   2. 522775 by 24   3. 255850 by 31
4. 2522456 by 87   5. 363861 by 21   6. 247558 by 61
7. 268591 by 35   8. 5281405 by 44   9. 1585075 by 39

B. **Divide to find the quotient and the remainder :**
10. 196128 by 38   11. 260034 by 59   12. 247738 by 53
13. 137458 by 225   14. 225489 by 28   15. 558946 by 115
16. 6586694 by 425   17. 865493 by 564   18. 2345200 by 96
19. 3431131 by 531   20. 4759375 by 642   21. 8913478 by 225
22. 2839115 by 766   23. 1889016 by 187   24. 4399909 by 526
25. 1032242 by 395   26. 4610918 by 526   27. 897684 by 427
28. 5436637 by 694   29. 7708480 by 416   30. 9999999 by 432
31. 628445 by 615   32. 5808154 by 446   33. 6987688 by 723

34. Write the correct figure in place of each square :

(a)
```
        □59□
   27 ) 969457
      - 81
        159
      - 1□5
        245
      - 243
         27
       - 27
          x
```

(b)
```
          7□078
   123 ) 8742594
       - 861
         132
       - 1□3
          959
        - 861
           9□4
         - 984
            X
```

35. A transport company earmarked Rs. 9606080 for buying 110 trucks. Find the cost of 1 truck.

36. Write the greatest number of seven digits and divide it by 416.

37. 462 VCRs were bought for Rs. 7708470. Find the cost of one VCR.

38. A packet can hold 144 ball-point pens. How many packets are required to pack 3698640 ball-point pens ?

6 | FACTORS AND MULTIPLES

A. Factors

We can arrange 2 tops like this :

We can describe this array with multiplication sentences :

$$1 \times 2 = 2 \qquad 2 \times 1 = 2$$

We can say that 1 and 2 are **factors** of 2.
We can also say that 2 is the **product** of 1 and 2.

We can arrange a set of 6 balls like this :

$$2 \times 3 = 6$$
$$3 \times 2 = 6$$

2 and 3 are **factors** of 6.
6 is the **product** of 2 and 3.

The set of 6 balls can also be arranged like this :

$$1 \times 6 = 6$$
$$6 \times 1 = 6$$

1 and 6 are **factors** of 6.
6 is the **product** of 1 and 6.

The set of 6 balls can be arranged in only
2 different rectangular arrays.
1, 2, 3 and 6 are all factors of 6.

Factors of a number can divide the number exactly.
1, 2, 3 and 6 can divide 6 exactly.
5 cannot divide 6 exactly.
5 is not a factor of 6.
4 cannot divide 6 exactly.
4 is not a factor of 6.

Any number can be shown to be a **product** of two of its **factors.** We can arrange 4 apples in these 2 ways :

$$2 \times 2 = 4 \qquad\qquad 4 \times 1 = 4$$

1, 2 and 4 are factors of 4.

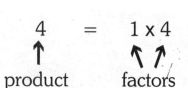

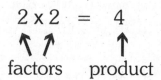

$$4 = 1 \times 4 \qquad\qquad 2 \times 2 = 4$$

product   factors   factors   product

1. **Name the factors in each of these.**

   (a) $2 \times 3 = 6$ (b) $4 \times 2 = 8$ (c) $5 = 1 \times 5$

   (d) $12 = 2 \times 6$ (e) $14 = 7 \times 2$ (f) $3 \times 5 = 15$

   (g) $16 = 2 \times 8$ (h) $24 = 6 \times 4$ (i) $7 \times 3 = 21$

2. **Name the missing factor in each of these.**

   (a) ___ $\times 5 = 10$ (b) $3 \times$ ___ $= 12$ (c) ___ $\times 7 = 7$

   (d) ___ $\times 4 = 16$ (e) $2 \times$ ___ $= 16$ (f) $4 \times$ ___ $= 20$

   (g) $9 \times$ ___ $= 18$ (h) ___ $\times 2 = 14$ (i) $5 \times$ ___ $= 15$

B. **Finding the factors of a number**

We can find all the factors of 12 like this :

Arranging 12 crosses in all possible rectangular arrays we have :

         x x x x $3 \times 4 = 12$

         x x x x   3 and 4 are factors of 12.

         x x x x

       x x x x x x $2 \times 6 = 12$

       x x x x x x   2 and 6 are factors of 12.

x x x x x x x x x x x x $1 \times 12 = 12$

           1 and 12 are factors of 12.

12 crosses can be arranged in only 3 different rectangular arrays.

1,2,3,4,6 and 12 are all factors of 12.

1. **Do these.**

(a)
1 x 7 = 7
The factors of 7 are _____.

(b) ★ ★ ★
1 x 3 = 3
The factors of 3 are _____.

(c) ▲▲▲▲ ▲▲▲▲▲▲▲▲
   ▲▲▲▲
2 x 4 = 8
The factors of 8 are _____.

(d) ▲ ▲ ▲ ▲ ▲
1 x 5 = 5
The factors of 5 are _____.

(e)
1 x 9 = 9
The factors of 9 are _____.

3 x 3 = 9

2. **Arrange the following number of beads in as many rectangular arrays as possible.**

(a) 10   (b) 11   (c) 14   (d) 15
(e) 16   (f) 18   (g) 20   (h) 24

3. **Fill up the missing factors.**

Product	Factors	Product	Factors
10	l,__,__,10.	16	l,__,__,__,16.
11	1,__.	18	1,__,__,__,__,18.
14	l,__,__,14.	20	1,__,__,__,__,20.
I5	l,__,__,15.	24	1,__,__,__,__,__, 12, 24.

4. **How many factors has each of these numbers ?**

(a) 2   (b) 3   (c) 5   (d) 7   (e) 11

Is a number always a factor of itself ?

What is the number that is a factor of every number ?

5. **What is the number that is a factor of every number ?**

C. Common factors
Look at these :

2 x 2 = 4
2 is a factor of 4

2 x 4 = 8
2 is a factor of 8

4 x 1 = 4
4 is a factor of 4

4 x 2 = 8
4 is a factor of 8

1, 2 and 4 are factors of 4. 1,2,4 and 8 are factors of 8.

   1, 2 and 4 are factors of both 4 and 8.

   1, 2 and 4 are **common factors** of 4 and 8.

4 is the largest number that is a factor of both 4 and 8.

We say 4 is the **greatest (highest) common factor** of 4 and 8.

It means that 4 is the biggest number that can divide 4 and 8.

Factors of 8 and 12

The factors of 8 are   **1**, **2**, **4*** and 8.

The factors of 12 are **1**, **2**, **3**, 4* 6, and 12.

8 is a factor of 8. It is not a factor of 12.

3, 6 and 12 are factors of 12. They are not factors of 8.

1, 2 and 4 are factors of both 8 and 12.

1, 2 and 4 are **common factors** of 8 and 12.

4 is the **highest common factor** of 8 and 12.

Common factor can be written **C.F.** for short.

Highest common factor can be written **H.C.F.** for short.

1.   The factors of 16 are **1**, **2**, **4***, 8, and 16.
   The factors of 20 are **1**, **2**, **4***, 5, 10 and 20.
   (a)   What are the common factors of 16 and 20 ?
   (b)   What is the highest common factor of 16 and 20 ?
   (c)   What are factors of 20 only and not of 16 ?

2. The factors of 18 are 1, 2*, 3, 6, 9 and 18.

The factors of 32 are 1, 2*, 4, 8, 16 and 32.

(a) What are the common factors of 18 and 32 ?

(b) What is the highest common factor of 18 and 32 ?

Example (1) : Find the common factors and the highest common factor of 24 and 36.

The factors of 24 are 1, 2, 3, 4, 6, 8, 12* and 24.

The factors of 36 are 1, 2, 3, 4, 6, 9, 12*, 18 and 36.

The CFs of 24 and 36 are 1, 2, 3, 4, 6 and 12.

The H.C.F. of 24 and 36 is 12.

Example (2) : Find the common factors and the highest common factor of 20 and 30.

The factors of 20 are 1, 2, 4, 5, 10* and 20.

The factors of 30 are 1, 2, 3, 5, 6, 10*, 15 and 30.

The CFs of 20 and 30 are 1, 2, 5 and 10.

The H.C.F. of 20 and 30 is 10.

3. Find the common factors and the highest common factors of the following :

(a) 4 and 6   (b) 6 and 8   (c) 4 and 12

(d) 6 and 12   (e) 5 and 10   (f) 9 and 12

(g) 4 and 10   (h) 8 and 16   (i) 12 and 15

(j) 6 and 18   (k) 10 and 15   (l) 9 and 18

(m) 14 and 21   (n) 12 and 24   (o) 10 and 20

(p) 18 and 24   (q) 10 and 30   (r) 25 and 35

D. Multiples

Count in ones.

•	••	•••	••••	•••••
1 x 1	1 x 2	1 x 3	1 x 4	1 x 5
1	2	3	4	5

1, 2, 3, 4, 5 are called **multiples** of 1.

To find multiples of 1, we write down 1, and add 1 each time. Every number has a countless number of multiples.

Count in twos.

oo	oo oo	ooo ooo	oooo oooo	ooooo ooooo
2 x 1	2 x 2	2 x 3	2 x 4	2 x 5
2	4	6	8	10

2, 4, 6, 8, 10 are called **multiples** of 2.

To find multiples of 2, we write down 2, and add 2 each time.

Count in threes.

o o o	oo oo oo	ooo ooo ooo	oooo oooo oooo	ooooo ooooo ooooo
3 x 1	3 x 2	3 x 3	3 x 4	3 x 5
3	6	9	12	15

3, 6, 9, 12, 15 are called **multiples** of 3.

To find multiples of 3, we write down 3, and add 3 each time.

The chart below shows the first ten multiples of 1, 2, 3, 4, 5 and 6.

X	1	2	3	4	5	6	7	8	9	10
1	1	2	3	4	5	6	7	8	9	10
2	2	4	6	8	10	12	14	16	18	20
3	3	6	9	12	15	18	21	24	27	30
4	4	8	12	16	20	24	28	32	36	40
5	5	10	15	20	25	30	35	40	45	50
6	6	12	18	24	30	36	42	48	54	60

6 is a **multiple** of 2.

6 is also a **multiple** of 3.

We say that 6 is a **common multiple** of 2 and 3.

From the chart on page 40 we see that 6, 12, and 18 are common multiples of 2 and 3.

Use the chart to answer these.

1. Write the first six multiples of 4.
2. Write the first six multiples of 5.
3. Write the first seven multiples of 6.
4. What are the common multiples of 2 and 4 ?
5. What are the common multiples of 3 and 6 ?
6. What are the common multiples of 2 and 6 ?
7. What are the common multiples of 3 and 5 ?
8. What are the common multiples of 2 and 3 ?

Look at this rectangular array :

 We can write addition and multiplication sentences for this array :

$3 + 3 + 3 + 3 + 3 = 15$ $5 + 5 + 5 = 15$

$5 \times 3 = 15$ $3 \times 5 = 15$

This array shows that 3 and 5 are factors of 15. It also shows that 15 is a multiple of 3, and 15 is a multiple of 5.

9. **Write multiplication sentences for each array and complete.**

a.

● ● ● ● ● ●
● ● ● ● ● ●

12 is a multiple of _____.
12 is a multiple of _____.

b.

X X X X X X X X X
X X X X X X X X X

18 is a multiple of _____.
18 is a multiple of _____.

c.

X X X X
X X X X
X X X X

12 is a multiple of _____.
12 is a multiple of _____.

d.

18 is a multiple of _____.
18 is a multiple of _____.

E. Lowest Common Multiple

The multiples of 2 are 2, 4, 6, 8, 10, 12, 14, 16, 18, ...
The multiples of 3 are 3, 6, 9, 12, 15, 18, 21, 24, 27, ...
The common multiples of 2 and 3 are 6, 12, 18, ...
6 is the smallest number which is a common multiple of 2 and 3.
6 is called the **lowest common multiple** of 2 and 3.
The lowest common multiple is written **L.C.M.** for short.

Write the first ten multiples of each of the following pairs of numbers and find the common multiples and the lowest common multiple.

1. (a) 2 and 4   (b) 3 and 4   (c) 2 and 5   (d) 2 and 6
2. (a) 3 and 5   (b) 4 and 5   (c) 3 and 5   (d) 4 and 6

3. (a) 4 and 8   (b) 3 and 9   (c) 6 and 8   (d) 5 and 10

4. (a) 3 and 12   (b) 4 and 12   (c) 6 and 12   (d) 8 and 12

5. Here is a set of numbers.

8, 10, 12, 14, 18, 21, 24, 27, 30, 32, 36

Which of these numbers are multiples of :
(a) 2   (b) 3   (c) 4   (d) 5
(e) 6   (f) 7   (g) 8   (h) 9

F. More exercises on factors and multiples

8 x 4 = 32   8 is a factor of 32.
4 is a factor of 32.
32 is the product of 8 and 4.
32 is a multiple of 8.
32 is a multiple of 4.

G. Fill up each blank with the correct word from below.

factor	multiple	product

1. (a) 5 x 7 = 35   5 is a _____ of 35.
    (b) 9 x 3 = 27   27 is the _____ of 9 and 3.
    (c) 6 x 8 = 48   48 is a _____ of 6.

2. **Circle the numbers which are factors of 32.**
    3, 4, 9, 10, 16, 20.

3. **Here are 5 numbers : 16, 32, 35, 44, 50.**
    Which of these have 4 as a factor ?

4. **Circle the numbers which are multiples of 6.**
    15, 18, 20, 24, 28, 36

5. **Complete the following multiples of 3 and 6.**
    Multiples of 3 : 3 ☐ ☐ ☐ ☐ ☐ ☐ 24 ......
    Multiples of 6 : 6 ☐ ☐ ☐ ☐ ☐ ☐ 48 ......

    (a) Use the above multiples of 3 and 6 to write down
        the common multiples of 3 and 6.
    (b) Name the lowest common multiple of 3 and 6.

6. **Here are 5 numbers: 2, 4, 6, 9, 12.**
    Circle the highest common factor of 18 and 24.

7. **Fill up the blanks.**
    (a) The factors of 3 are __ and __.
    (b) The only factor of 1 is __.
    (c) The product of 6 and 3 is __.
    (d) 6 is a multiple of 2 and __.
    (e) The lowest common multiple of 3 and 4 is __.

8. **Complete the following factors of 12 and 24.**
    Factors of 12: 1 ☐ ☐ ☐ ☐ 12.
    Factors of 24: 1 ☐ ☐ ☐ ☐ ☐ ☐ 24.
    (a) Name the common factors of 12 and 24.
    (b) What is the highest common factor of 12 and 24 ?

9. **What are the factors of 35 ?**

7 MORE ABOUT FRACTIONS

A. Mixed numbers

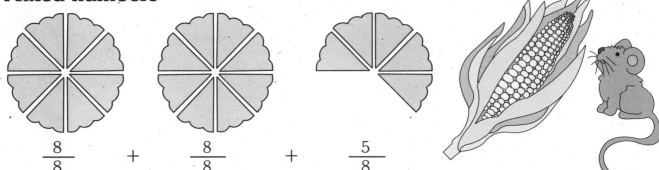

$$\frac{8}{8} \quad + \quad \frac{8}{8} \quad + \quad \frac{5}{8}$$

The picture above shows 21 pieces of cake. Each piece is $\frac{1}{8}$ of a cake. There are 2 whole cakes and $\frac{5}{8}$ of a cake.

$$\frac{8}{8} + \frac{8}{8} + \frac{5}{8} = \frac{21}{8} = 2 + \frac{5}{8} = 2\frac{5}{8}$$

An improper fraction can be expressed as a mixed number, A mixed number is the sum of a whole number and a proper fraction.

Study the pictures below.

(a) To change an improper fraction to a mixed number.

(b) To change a mixed number to an improper fraction.

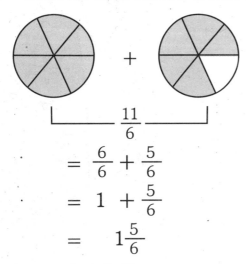

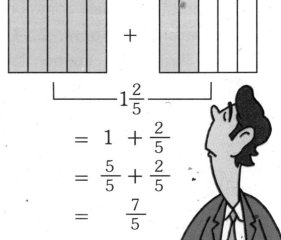

$$+ \quad \frac{11}{6}$$

$$= \frac{6}{6} + \frac{5}{6}$$

$$= 1 + \frac{5}{6}$$

$$= 1\frac{5}{6}$$

$$+ \quad 1\frac{2}{5}$$

$$= 1 + \frac{2}{5}$$

$$= \frac{5}{5} + \frac{2}{5}$$

$$= \frac{7}{5}$$

1. **Change the following to mixed numbers.**
   (a) $\frac{7}{6}$ (b) $\frac{11}{8}$ (c) $\frac{7}{4}$ (d) $\frac{9}{5}$ (e) $\frac{15}{8}$ (f) $\frac{17}{12}$

2. **Change the following to improper fractions.**
   (a) $1\frac{1}{2}$ (b) $1\frac{3}{4}$ (c) $1\frac{1}{5}$ (d) $2\frac{1}{2}$ (e) $2\frac{1}{8}$ (f) $2\frac{2}{12}$

B. Addition and subtraction of like fractions

Fractions that have the same denominators are known as **like fractions**.

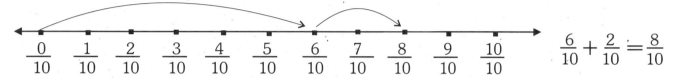

$$\frac{4}{10} + \frac{3}{10} = \frac{7}{10}$$

$$\frac{6}{10} + \frac{2}{10} = \frac{8}{10}$$

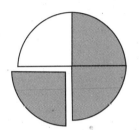 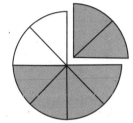

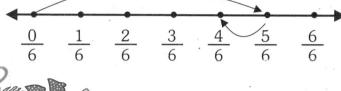

$$\frac{3}{4} - \frac{1}{4} = \frac{2}{4}$$

$$\frac{6}{8} - \frac{2}{8} = \frac{4}{8}$$

$$\frac{5}{6} - \frac{1}{6} = \frac{4}{6}$$

Look at these :

(1) $\frac{3}{8} - \frac{1}{8} = \frac{4}{8}$

$= \frac{4}{8} \div \frac{4}{4}$

$= \frac{1}{2}$

(2) $\frac{9}{10} - \frac{7}{10} = \frac{2}{10}$

$= \frac{2}{10} \div \frac{2}{2}$

$= \frac{1}{5}$

Now do these.

1. (a) $\frac{1}{10} + \frac{3}{10} + \frac{1}{10} =$ (b) $\frac{1}{8} + \frac{5}{8} + \frac{1}{8} =$ (c) $\frac{5}{12} + \frac{1}{12} + \frac{5}{12} =$

2. (a) $\frac{2}{15} + \frac{4}{15} + \frac{7}{15} =$ (b) $\frac{4}{9} + \frac{1}{9} + \frac{1}{9} =$ (c) $\frac{1}{15} + \frac{4}{15} + \frac{7}{15} =$

3. (a) $\frac{7}{10} + \frac{3}{10} =$ (b) $\frac{7}{10} + \frac{3}{10} =$ (c) $\frac{8}{15} - \frac{2}{15} =$

4. (a) $\frac{3}{4} - \frac{3}{4} =$ (b) $\frac{3}{4} - \frac{3}{4} =$ (c) $\frac{5}{9} - \frac{2}{9} =$

5. (a) $\frac{5}{8} - \frac{3}{8} =$ (b) $\frac{5}{8} - \frac{3}{8} =$ (c) $\frac{7}{16} - \frac{5}{16} =$

6. (a) $\frac{2}{9} + \frac{1}{9} =$ (b) $\frac{2}{9} + \frac{1}{9} =$ (c) $\frac{8}{15} + \frac{3}{15} =$

7. (a) $\frac{7}{21} - \frac{5}{21} =$ (b) $\frac{7}{21} - \frac{5}{21} =$ (c) $\frac{13}{14} - \frac{7}{24} =$

8. (a) $\frac{17}{21} - \frac{10}{21} =$ (b) $\frac{17}{21} - \frac{10}{21} =$ (c) $\frac{14}{15} - \frac{4}{15} =$

C. Addition and subtraction of unlike fractions

Fractions that have different denominators are known as **unlike fractions.**

How do we add or subtract unlike fractions ? First we change the unlike fractions to like fractions. Then we add or subtract the fractions. We can show the addition of ¼ and ¾ in two ways.

(1)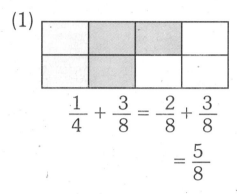

$$\frac{1}{4} + \frac{3}{8} = \frac{2}{8} + \frac{3}{8}$$

$$= \frac{5}{8}$$

(2)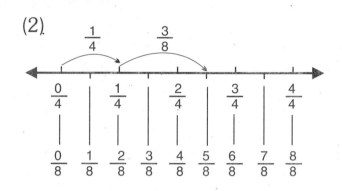

We can show the subtraction of $\frac{1}{2}$ from $\frac{7}{8}$ in two ways also.

(1)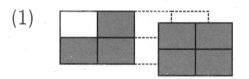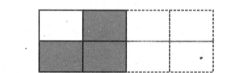

$$\frac{7}{8} - \frac{1}{2} = \frac{7}{8} - \frac{4}{8} = \frac{3}{8}$$

(2)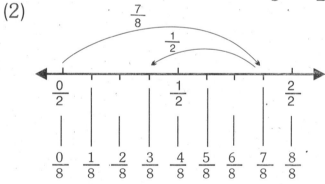

$$\frac{7}{8} - \frac{1}{2} = \frac{7}{8} - \frac{4}{8}$$

$$= \frac{3}{8}$$

Rename the fractions in terms of the same denominator and then find their sums or their differences.

(1) (a) $\frac{1}{4} + \frac{3}{8} = \frac{\square}{8} + \frac{3}{8} =$ (b) $\frac{1}{3} + \frac{2}{9} = \frac{\square}{9} + \frac{2}{9} =$

(2) (a) $\frac{1}{5} - \frac{1}{10} = \frac{\square}{10} - \frac{1}{10} =$ (b) $\frac{1}{3} - \frac{1}{9} = \frac{\square}{9} - \frac{1}{9} =$

(3) (a) $\frac{3}{4} - \frac{1}{2} = \frac{3}{4} - \frac{\square}{4} =$ (b) $\frac{2}{5} + \frac{3}{10} = \frac{\square}{10} + \frac{3}{10} =$

D. Addition and subtraction of unlike fractions

(1) We want to find the sum : $\frac{1}{2} + \frac{1}{3}$.

We build a table of equivalent fractions for $\frac{1}{2}$ and $\frac{1}{3}$.

$$\frac{1}{2} = \frac{2}{4} = \frac{3}{6} = \frac{4}{8} = \frac{5}{10} = \frac{6}{12} = \dots\dots\dots\dots$$

$$\frac{1}{3} = \frac{2}{6} = \frac{3}{6} = \frac{4}{9} = \frac{5}{12} = \dots\dots\dots\dots$$

We choose the equivalent fractions of $\frac{1}{2}$ and $\frac{1}{3}$ that have the same denominator. We then change $\frac{1}{2}$ and $\frac{1}{3}$ to sixths or twelfths. It is better to choose the equivalent fractions with the smaller denominator.

$$\frac{1}{2} + \frac{1}{3} = \frac{3}{6} + \frac{2}{6} = \frac{5}{6} .$$

(2) We want to find the difference : $\frac{1}{3} - \frac{1}{4}$

Rename $\frac{1}{3}$ and $\frac{1}{4}$ so that they have a common denominator.

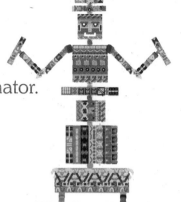

$$\frac{1}{3} = \frac{2}{6} = \frac{3}{9} = \frac{4}{12} = \dots\dots\dots\dots$$

$$\frac{1}{4} = \frac{2}{8} = \frac{3}{12} = \dots\dots\dots\dots$$

$$\frac{1}{3} - \frac{1}{4} = \frac{4}{12} - \frac{3}{12} = \frac{1}{12} .$$

Rename the fractions in terms of the same denominator. Find their sums or differences.

1. (a) $\frac{1}{2} + \frac{1}{5} = $ —— (b) $\frac{1}{4} + \frac{1}{3} = $ —— (c) $\frac{1}{3} + \frac{1}{5} = $ ——

2. (a) $\frac{1}{4} + \frac{2}{3} = $ —— (b) $\frac{2}{5} + \frac{1}{2} = $ —— (c) $\frac{1}{3} + \frac{1}{2} = $ ——

3. (a) $\frac{2}{5} + \frac{1}{3} = $ —— (b) $\frac{1}{5} + \frac{1}{4} = $ —— (c) $\frac{3}{4} + \frac{1}{5} = $ ——

4. (a) $\frac{2}{5} + \frac{1}{5} = $ —— (b) $\frac{2}{5} + \frac{1}{4} = $ —— (c) $\frac{3}{5} + \frac{1}{3} = $ ——

5. (a) $\frac{1}{2} - \frac{1}{5} = $ —— (b) $\frac{1}{2} - \frac{1}{5} = $ —— (c) $\frac{2}{3} - \frac{1}{4} = $ ——

6. (a) $\frac{2}{3} - \frac{1}{2} = $ —— (b) $\frac{1}{4} - \frac{1}{5} = $ —— (c) $\frac{2}{3} - \frac{1}{8} = $ ——

7. (a) $\frac{3}{4} - \frac{1}{3} = $ —— (b) $\frac{2}{5} - \frac{1}{4} = $ —— (c) $\frac{3}{4} - \frac{2}{4} = $ ——

8. (a) $\frac{1}{2} - \frac{2}{5} = $ —— (b) $\frac{3}{4} - \frac{2}{5} = $ —— (c) $\frac{3}{5} - \frac{1}{2} = $ ——

9. (a) $\frac{3}{4} - \frac{3}{5} = $ —— (b) $\frac{4}{5} - \frac{1}{2} = $ —— (c) $\frac{4}{5} - \frac{3}{4} = $ ——

E. Addition with mixed numbers

The addition of mixed numbers can be shown with diagrams.

(1) 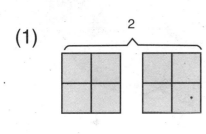 +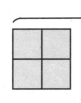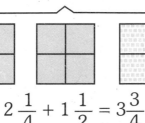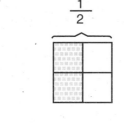

$$2\frac{1}{4} + 1\frac{1}{2} = 3\frac{3}{4}$$

(2)
$$2\frac{1}{4} + 3\frac{5}{8} = 2\frac{2}{8} + 3\frac{5}{8}$$
$$= 5\frac{7}{8}$$
$$= 5\frac{7}{8}$$

Explanation

We rename as $\frac{1}{4}$ as $\frac{2}{8}$ ($\frac{1}{4} = \frac{2}{8} = \dots$)

We add the whole numbers : $2+3=5$

We add the fractions : $\frac{2}{8} = \frac{5}{8} = \frac{7}{8}$

Now do these.

    (a)   (b)   (c)

1. $1\frac{1}{4} + 2\frac{4}{1} =$ $1\frac{1}{8} + 1\frac{3}{8} =$ $2\frac{1}{3} + 1\frac{1}{3} =$

2. $1\frac{1}{2} + 1\frac{1}{4} =$ $1\frac{1}{4} + 1\frac{1}{8} =$ $1\frac{1}{3} + 1\frac{1}{6} =$

3.
$$\begin{array}{r} 15\frac{1}{2} \\ +21\frac{1}{4} \\ \hline \\ \hline \end{array}$$
$$\begin{array}{r} 24\frac{1}{5} \\ +31\frac{3}{5} \\ \hline \\ \hline \end{array}$$
$$\begin{array}{r} 32\frac{1}{8} \\ +17\frac{1}{2} \\ \hline \\ \hline \end{array}$$

(3)

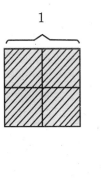 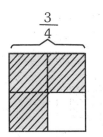 +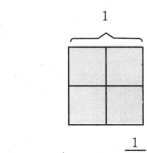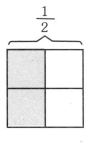

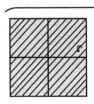 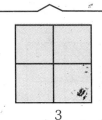 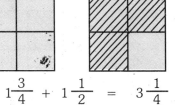 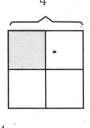

$$1\frac{3}{4} + 1\frac{1}{2} = 3\frac{1}{4}$$

(4) We want to find the sum : $2\frac{1}{2} + 1\frac{3}{4}$

$2\frac{1}{2} + 1\frac{3}{4}$

$= 2\frac{2}{4} + 1\frac{3}{4}$

$= 3\frac{5}{4}$

$= 3 + 1\frac{1}{4}$

$= 4\frac{1}{4}$

Explanation

We rename $\frac{1}{2}$ as $\frac{2}{4}$. $\left(\frac{1}{2}, \frac{2}{4}, ...\right)$

We add the whole numbers : $2 + 1 = 3$

We add the fractions: $\frac{2}{4} + \frac{3}{4} = \frac{5}{4}$

We change $\frac{5}{4}$ to mixed numbers :

$\frac{5}{4} = 1\frac{1}{4}$.

Now do these.

  (a)   (b)   (c)

1. $1\frac{1}{2} + 1\frac{5}{8} =$ $2\frac{1}{3} + 1\frac{5}{6} =$ $3\frac{1}{2} + 1\frac{5}{6} =$

2. $2\frac{2}{3} + 3\frac{5}{6} =$ $2\frac{7}{8} + 1\frac{1}{8} =$ $2\frac{7}{8} + 1\frac{1}{2} =$

3. $1\frac{3}{4} + 2\frac{3}{8} =$ $2\frac{2}{8} + 3\frac{3}{4} =$ $3\frac{3}{4} + 1\frac{7}{8} =$

4. $15\frac{1}{2}$ $36\frac{3}{8}$ $58\frac{1}{2}$

   $+17\frac{1}{4}$ $+45\frac{3}{4}$ $+43\frac{3}{8}$

  ————   ————   ————

  ————   ————   ————

F. Subtraction with mixed numbers.

The subtraction of mixed numbers can also be shown with diagrams.

(1)

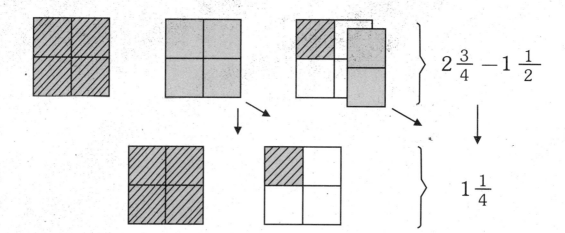

$2\frac{3}{4} - 1\frac{1}{2}$

$1\frac{1}{4}$

(2)

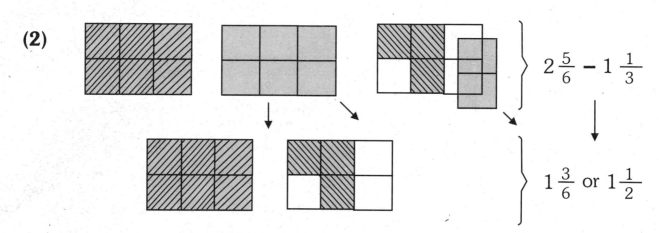

$2\frac{5}{6} - 1\frac{1}{3}$

$1\frac{3}{6}$ or $1\frac{1}{2}$

(3)

$$7\frac{7}{8} - 4\frac{3}{4} = 7\frac{7}{8} - 4\frac{6}{8}$$
$$= 3\frac{1}{8}$$

Explanation

We rename $\frac{3}{4}$ as $\frac{6}{8}$ $\left(\frac{3}{4} = \frac{6}{8} = ...\right)$

We subtract the whole numbers :

$7 - 4 = 3$

We subtract the fractions : $\frac{7}{8} - \frac{6}{8} = \frac{1}{8}$

Now do these.

	(a)	(b)	(c)
1.	$3\frac{3}{4} - 1\frac{1}{4} =$	$2\frac{5}{8} - 1\frac{3}{8} =$	$3\frac{5}{6} - 2\frac{1}{6} =$
2.	$3\frac{1}{2} - 2\frac{1}{4} =$	$2\frac{3}{4} - 1\frac{1}{2} =$	$3\frac{1}{2} - 1\frac{1}{8} =$

3.

$$25\tfrac{1}{2}$$
$$-14\tfrac{1}{4}$$
_____

$$30\tfrac{3}{4}$$
$$-20\tfrac{1}{8}$$
_____

$$26\tfrac{6}{8}$$
$$-14\tfrac{1}{4}$$
_____

$$42\tfrac{5}{6}$$
$$-31\tfrac{1}{3}$$
_____

4.

$$46\tfrac{7}{8}$$
$$-29\tfrac{1}{8}$$
_____

$$53\tfrac{5}{6}$$
$$-19\tfrac{2}{3}$$
_____

$$75\tfrac{3}{4}$$
$$-49\tfrac{3}{8}$$
_____

$$66\tfrac{5}{8}$$
$$-28\tfrac{1}{4}$$
_____

(4) We want to find the difference : $3\tfrac{1}{4} - 1\tfrac{1}{2}$

$$3\tfrac{1}{4} - 1\tfrac{1}{2} = 3\tfrac{1}{4} - 1\tfrac{2}{3}$$
$$= 2\tfrac{5}{4} - 1\tfrac{2}{4}$$
$$= 1\tfrac{3}{4}$$

Explanation

$\tfrac{2}{4}$ cannot be subtracted from $\tfrac{1}{4}$.
So, change $3\tfrac{1}{4}$ to $2\tfrac{5}{4}$

$\left(3\tfrac{1}{4} - 2 + \tfrac{4}{4} + \tfrac{1}{4} = 2\tfrac{5}{4}\right)$

(5) We want to find the difference : $3\tfrac{1}{3} - 1\tfrac{5}{6}$

$$3\tfrac{1}{3} - 1\tfrac{5}{6}$$
$$= 3\tfrac{2}{6} - 1\tfrac{5}{6}$$
$$= 2\tfrac{8}{6} - 1\tfrac{5}{6}$$
$$= 1\tfrac{3}{6}$$
$$= 1\tfrac{1}{2}$$

Explanation

We rename $\tfrac{1}{3}$ as $\tfrac{2}{6}$. $(\tfrac{1}{3}, \tfrac{2}{6}, \ldots\ldots)$
We change $3\tfrac{2}{6}$ to $2\tfrac{8}{6}$. $(3\tfrac{2}{6} = 2 + \tfrac{6}{6} + \tfrac{2}{6} = 2\tfrac{8}{6})$
We subtract the whole numbers : $2-1=1$.
We subtract the fractions : $\tfrac{8}{6} - \tfrac{5}{6} = \tfrac{3}{6}$.
We rename $\tfrac{3}{6}$ as $\tfrac{1}{2}$.

Now do these.

	(a)	(b)	(c)
1.	$3\tfrac{1}{4} - 1\tfrac{3}{4} =$	$4\tfrac{1}{8} - 1\tfrac{3}{8} =$	$3\tfrac{1}{6} - 1\tfrac{5}{6} =$
2.	$4\tfrac{1}{3} - 2\tfrac{2}{3} =$	$3\tfrac{3}{8} - 1\tfrac{5}{8} =$	$4\tfrac{1}{8} - 2\tfrac{5}{8} =$
3.	$4\tfrac{1}{4} - 2\tfrac{1}{4} =$	$5\tfrac{1}{8} - 2\tfrac{1}{4} =$	$4\tfrac{1}{6} - 1\tfrac{1}{3} =$
4.	$5\tfrac{1}{6} - 2\tfrac{1}{2} =$	$4\tfrac{1}{4} - 1\tfrac{3}{8} =$	$3\tfrac{1}{2} - 1\tfrac{5}{8} =$

It's not this easy.

G. Addition and subtraction problems

Example : A boy swam for $1\frac{1}{2}$ hours in the morning and $1\frac{5}{6}$ hours in the evening. How many hours did he swim altogether ?

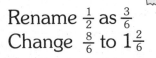

In the morning he swam for $1\frac{1}{2}$ h.

In the evening he swam for $1\frac{5}{6}$ h.

Rename $\frac{1}{2}$ as $\frac{3}{6}$

Change $\frac{8}{6}$ to $1\frac{2}{6}$

Altogether he swam for $1\frac{1}{2}$ h $+ 1\frac{5}{6}$ h

$= \left(1\frac{3}{6} + 1\frac{5}{6}\right)$ h

$= 2\frac{8}{6}$ h $= 3\frac{2}{6}$ h $= 3\frac{1}{3}$ h.

Do these.

1. Sanjay spent $\frac{3}{4}$ hour reading and $\frac{1}{4}$ hour doing mathematics. How much time did he spend studying altogether ?

2. The journey from Anil's house to Red Fort took $1\frac{1}{4}$ hours. The return journey by a different route took $1\frac{1}{2}$ hours. How long did the two journeys take ?

3. A plank is $1\frac{1}{3}$ metres long. Another plank is $1\frac{1}{6}$ metres long. What is the total length of the two planks ?

4. Prasanti bought two pieces of material. One piece is $1\frac{1}{4}$ metres and the other is $1\frac{3}{8}$ metres. How much material did she buy ?

5. A piece of rope is $4\frac{3}{5}$ metres long. It is cut into two parts. One part is $1\frac{2}{5}$ metres long. What is the length of the other part ?

6. A bucket of sand weighs $12\frac{1}{2}$ kilograms. A bucket of cement weighs $9\frac{1}{4}$ kilograms. How much heavier is the bucket of sand than the bucket of cement ?

7. Abanti weighs $33\frac{1}{3}$ kilograms. Auranti weighs $25\frac{1}{6}$ kilograms. What is the difference in their weight ?

8. A man took 18 minutes to row from one island to another. His return journey took $25\frac{5}{8}$ minutes. How much longer did he take to row on his return journey ?

9. Mary used $2\frac{3}{4}$ cups of sugar and $7\frac{1}{2}$ cups of flour for making a cake. How many cups of flour and sugar did she use altogether ?

10. A can contains $22\frac{1}{2}$ litres of oil. Mr. Gupta uses up $15\frac{1}{4}$ litres of oil from the can. How many litres of oil does the can contain now ?

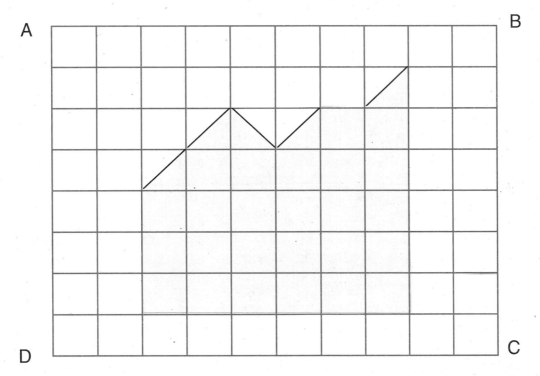

11. Find the area of the rectangle ABCD by counting and adding the number of small squares. Find the area of the shaded part of the rectangle in the same way. Find the area of the unshaded part of the rectangle ABCD without counting the small squares.

12. Rahman is $1\frac{1}{6}$ metres tall. His father is $\frac{2}{3}$ of a metre taller than him. What is his father's height ?

13. The height of the tallest boy in the class is $1\frac{3}{8}$ metres and that of the shortest boy is $\frac{3}{4}$ metre. What is the difference in their heights ?

14. A tailor bought $15\frac{1}{2}$ metres of ribbon. He used up $9\frac{1}{8}$ metres. How much ribbon had he left ?

15. A tank is full of water. Mary uses $\frac{1}{3}$ of it for watering the garden. What fraction of water still remains in the tank ?

H. Multiplication of a fraction by a whole number.

Look at the rectangle. It is divided into 8 equal parts. We can count the shaded parts. We say that three-eighths of the rectangle is shaded.

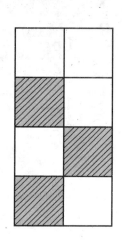

$$\frac{1}{8} + \frac{1}{8} + \frac{1}{8} = \frac{3}{8}$$

We can express this as three times one-eighth :

$$3 \times \frac{1}{8} = \frac{3}{8}$$

Look at the number line. It is marked in twelfths.

$$\frac{1}{12} + \frac{1}{12} + \frac{1}{12} + \frac{1}{12} + \frac{1}{12} + \frac{1}{12} + \frac{1}{12} = \frac{7}{12}$$

$$7 \times \frac{1}{12} = \frac{7}{12}$$

1. Complete these using the pictures.

(a)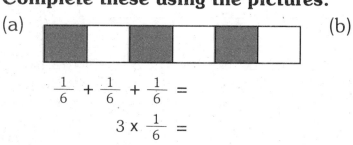

$$\frac{1}{6} + \frac{1}{6} + \frac{1}{6} =$$

$$3 \times \frac{1}{6} =$$

(b)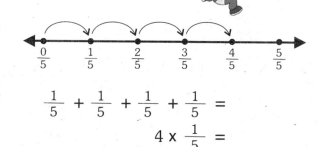

$$\frac{1}{5} + \frac{1}{5} + \frac{1}{5} + \frac{1}{5} =$$

$$4 \times \frac{1}{5} =$$

(c)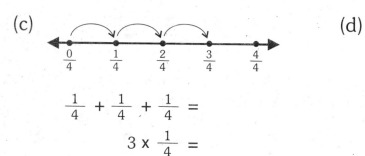

$$\frac{1}{4} + \frac{1}{4} + \frac{1}{4} =$$

$$3 \times \frac{1}{4} =$$

(d)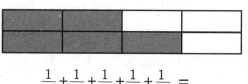

$$\frac{1}{8} + \frac{1}{8} + \frac{1}{8} + \frac{1}{8} + \frac{1}{8} =$$

$$5 \times \frac{1}{8} =$$

2. Now do these.

a. $\frac{1}{6} + \frac{1}{6} + \frac{1}{6} + \frac{1}{6} + \frac{1}{6} =$

$5 \times \frac{1}{6} =$

b. $\frac{1}{12} + \frac{1}{12} + \frac{1}{12} + \frac{1}{12} =$

$4 \times \frac{1}{12} =$

c. $\frac{1}{9} + \frac{1}{9} + \frac{1}{9} + \frac{1}{9} =$

$4 \times \frac{1}{9} =$

d. $\frac{1}{10} + \frac{1}{10} + \frac{1}{10} + \frac{1}{10} + \frac{1}{10} + \frac{1}{10} =$

$6 \times \frac{1}{10} =$

Look at these :

$$\frac{2}{3} + \frac{2}{3} + \frac{2}{3} + \frac{2}{3} + \frac{2}{3} = \frac{10}{3} = 3\frac{1}{3}$$

$$5 \times \frac{2}{3} = \frac{10}{3} = 3\frac{1}{3}$$

$$\frac{3}{4} + \frac{3}{4} + \frac{3}{4} + \frac{3}{4} + \frac{3}{4} + \frac{3}{4} = \frac{18}{4} = 4\frac{2}{4} = 4\frac{1}{4}$$

$$6 \times \frac{3}{4} = \frac{18}{4} = 4\frac{2}{4} = 4\frac{1}{4}$$

When multiplying a fraction by a whole number, multiply the numerator by the whole number. Then divide that result by the denominator.

3. **Use a number line or drawings to show each of the following.**

(a) $5 \times \frac{1}{2} =$ (b) $6 \times \frac{1}{4} =$ (c) $6 \times \frac{1}{5} =$

(d) $4 \times \frac{1}{3} =$ (e) $8 \times \frac{1}{4} =$ (f) $4 \times \frac{2}{5} =$

(g) $6 \times \frac{1}{3} =$ (h) $4 \times \frac{3}{5} =$ (i) $9 \times \frac{1}{8} =$

(j) $5 \times \frac{1}{4} =$ (k) $5 \times \frac{1}{5} =$ (l) $4 \times \frac{1}{2} =$

Now do these.

4. Sunita eats $\frac{1}{2}$ an apple a day. How many apples does she eat in 7 days ?

5. Priya drinks $\frac{1}{2}$ a cup of milk a day. How many cups of milk does she drink in 5 days ?

6. A piece of string is $\frac{1}{8}$ metre long. What is the total length of 5 such pieces of string ?

7. Kailash spends $\frac{1}{4}$ of an hour walking to and from school each day. How many hours would he spend in walking to and from school in 5 days ?

I. Fraction of a whole number

(a)

$\frac{1}{3}$ of a circle.

$\frac{1}{2}$

(b)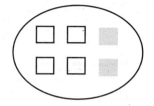

$\frac{1}{3}$ of a set of 6 squares.

Fractions can represent part of an object as in **(a)**.

Fractions can also represent a part of a set which is made up of several objects as in **(b)**.

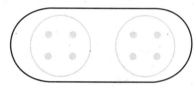

What is $\frac{1}{2}$ of 8 ?

This is a set of 8 marbles. It is separated into 2 equal groups ? Each group is $\frac{1}{2}$ of the set of 8 marbles. How many marbles are there in each group Now separate the set of 8 marbles into 4 equal groups. Each group is $\frac{1}{4}$ of the set of 8 marbles. How many marbles are there in each group now ?

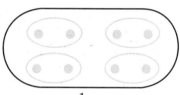

What is $\frac{1}{4}$ of 8 ?

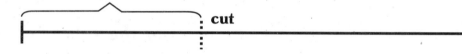

cut

This string is 15 cm long.

(a) Fold it into 3 equal parts and mark each part with your pen.

What fraction is each part ?

Each part is ⬚ of the 15 cm long string.

What fraction is 2 equal parts ?

Two equal parts is ⬚ of the 15 cm-long string.

(b) Cut out one part. Measure it.

One part is ⬚ cm long. What is $\frac{1}{3}$ of 15 cm ?

(c) Measure the remaining 2 equal parts.

Two parts is ⬚ cm long. What is $\frac{2}{3}$ of 15 cm ?

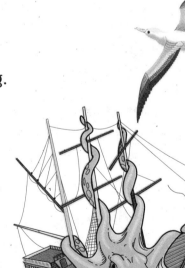

1. Complete these using the pictures.

(a)
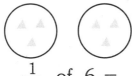
$\frac{1}{2}$ of 6 =

(b)

$\frac{1}{3}$ of 12 =

(c)
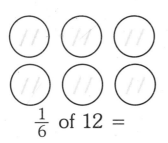
$\frac{1}{6}$ of 12 =

(d)
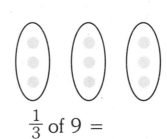
$\frac{1}{3}$ of 9 =

(e)

$\frac{1}{6}$ of 6 =

(f)
$\frac{1}{2}$ of 10 =

(g)
$\frac{1}{4}$ of 12 =

(h)
$\frac{1}{2}$ of 12 =

(i)
$\frac{1}{8}$ of 8 =

(j)
$\frac{1}{5}$ of 10 =

It help to read the instructions.

Look at this :

3 sets of 4 means 3 x 4

$\frac{1}{2}$ a set of 4 means $\frac{1}{2}$ x 4

$\frac{1}{2}$ x 4 = $\frac{1}{2}$ x $\frac{4}{1}$ = $\frac{1 \times 4}{2 \times 1}$

$= \frac{4}{2} = 2$

The working for $\frac{1}{2}$ x 4 can also be done in this way.

3 sets of 4

$\frac{1}{2}$ a set of 4

$\frac{1}{2}$ x 4 = $\frac{1}{2}$ x $\frac{4}{1}$ = $\frac{1 \times 4}{2 \times 1}$ = $\frac{1 \times 4}{1 \times 2}$ = $\frac{1}{1}$ x $\frac{4}{2}$

$= 1 \times 2 = 2$

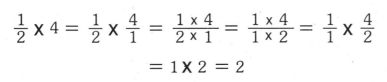

Look at this :

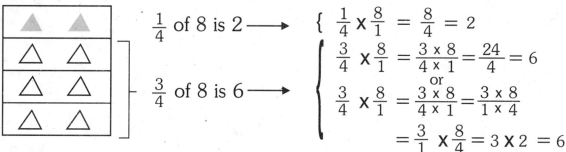

$\frac{1}{4}$ of 8 is 2 $\longrightarrow$ $\Big\{$ $\frac{1}{4} \times \frac{8}{1} = \frac{8}{4} = 2$

$\frac{3}{4} \times \frac{8}{1} = \frac{3 \times 8}{4 \times 1} = \frac{24}{4} = 6$

or

$\frac{3}{4}$ of 8 is 6 $\longrightarrow$ $\frac{3}{4} \times \frac{8}{1} = \frac{3 \times 8}{4 \times 1} = \frac{3 \times 8}{1 \times 4}$

$= \frac{3}{1} \times \frac{8}{4} = 3 \times 2 = 6$

2. Study the drawings and complete.

(a)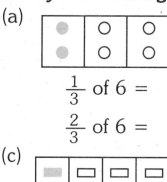

$\frac{1}{3}$ of 6 =

$\frac{2}{3}$ of 6 =

(b)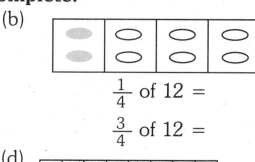

$\frac{1}{4}$ of 12 =

$\frac{3}{4}$ of 12 =

(c)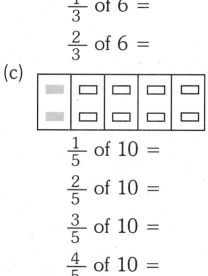

$\frac{1}{5}$ of 10 =

$\frac{2}{5}$ of 10 =

$\frac{3}{5}$ of 10 =

$\frac{4}{5}$ of 10 =

(d)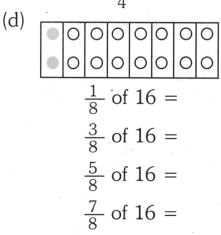

$\frac{1}{8}$ of 16 =

$\frac{3}{8}$ of 16 =

$\frac{5}{8}$ of 16 =

$\frac{7}{8}$ of 16 =

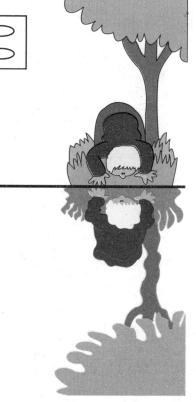

Find the value of :

3. (a) $\frac{1}{2}$ of 12 =   (b) $\frac{1}{3}$ of 15 =   (c) $\frac{1}{4}$ of 16 =

4. (a) $\frac{1}{5}$ of 15 =   (b) $\frac{1}{8}$ of 24 =   (c) $\frac{1}{9}$ of 18 =

5. (a) $\frac{2}{3}$ of 12 =   (b) $\frac{3}{4}$ of 20 =   (c) $\frac{2}{5}$ of 15 =

6. (a) $\frac{3}{5}$ of 20 =   (b) $\frac{3}{8}$ of 32 =   (c) $\frac{4}{5}$ of 35 =

7. (a) $\frac{2}{3}$ of 18 =   (b) $\frac{2}{5}$ of 40 =   (c) $\frac{3}{4}$ of 28 =

8. (a) $\frac{1}{2}$ of 24 =   (b) $\frac{2}{3}$ of 24 =   (c) $\frac{3}{5}$ of 45 =

9. (a) $\frac{1}{6}$ of 54 =   (b) $\frac{5}{8}$ of 56 =   (c) $\frac{3}{4}$ of 36 =

10. (a) $\frac{4}{5}$ of 40 =   (b) $\frac{3}{4}$ of 32 =   (c) $\frac{5}{6}$ of 48 =

11. (a) $\frac{3}{8}$ of 64 =   (b) $\frac{4}{5}$ of 50 =   (c) $\frac{5}{6}$ of 54 =

12. (a) $\frac{2}{5}$ of 50 =   (b) $\frac{8}{9}$ of 90 =   (c) $\frac{2}{9}$ of 27 =

J. Problems on fractions

Example (1) : What is $\frac{2}{3}$ of 21 metres ?

Solution : $\frac{2}{3}$ of 21 metres $= 2 \times \frac{21}{3}$ metres

$= 2 \times 7$ metres

$= 14$ metres

Example (2) : What is $\frac{2}{3}$ of 18 hours ?

Solution : $\frac{2}{3}$ of 18 hours $= 2 \times \frac{18}{3}$ hours

$= \frac{36}{3}$ hours

$= 12$ hours

Example (3) : In a class there are 36 pupils. $\frac{3}{4}$ of the pupils are boys. How many boys are there in the class ?

Solution : There are 36 pupils.

Number of boys $= \frac{3}{4}$ of 36

$= \frac{3 \times 36}{4 \times 4} = \frac{3 \times 36}{1 \times 4}$

$= \frac{3}{1} \times \frac{36}{4} = 3 \times 9$

$= 27$

I'm all mixed up!

Find the value of :

1.	(a) $\frac{1}{2}$ of Rs 36		(b) $\frac{2}{5}$ of 25 hours
2.	(a) $\frac{3}{5}$ of Rs 45		(b) $\frac{1}{6}$ of 54 centimetres
3.	(a) $\frac{3}{8}$ of 56 grams		(b) $\frac{3}{4}$ of 36 litres
4.	(a) $\frac{4}{5}$ of 40 minutes		(b) $\frac{3}{4}$ of 28 metres
5.	(a) $\frac{5}{8}$ of 64 seconds		(b) $\frac{2}{3}$ of Rs 21
6.	(a) $\frac{2}{5}$ of Rs 60		(b) $\frac{5}{8}$ of 72 litres
7.	(a) $\frac{1}{2}$ of 54 centimetres		(b) $\frac{1}{2}$ of Rs 96
8.	(a) $\frac{3}{5}$ of 15 grams		(b) $\frac{5}{8}$ of 56 litres
9.	(a) $\frac{5}{8}$ of 48 seconds		(b) $\frac{2}{3}$ of 42 hours
10.	(a) $\frac{5}{6}$ of 54 minutes		(b) $\frac{3}{8}$ of 40 grams

Do these.

11. There are 42 books on the table. $\frac{5}{6}$ of them are in a box on the table. How many books are there in the box ?

12. A girl spent $\frac{2}{3}$ of her Rs 21. How much did she spend ?

13. The tailor used $\frac{3}{4}$ of 12 metres of cloth. How much cloth did he use ?

14. A motorist used $\frac{3}{5}$ of 10 litres of petrol on a journey. How much petrol did he use ?

15. There are 72 library books in the classroom. $\frac{3}{8}$ the books are new. How many books are new ?

16. Gagan has 56 fishes. He keeps $\frac{7}{8}$ of them in a large tank and the rest in a small tank. How many fishes are kept in the large tank ?

K. General exercises on fractions.

1. Fill in the blanks with these words.

an object,   a set of objects,   mixed number,   whole number,

proper fraction,   numerator,   improper fraction,   denominator.

(a) $\frac{4}{8}$ is a —————————.

(b) $3\frac{1}{4}$ is a —————————.

(c) 4 is a —————————.

(d) $\frac{8}{3}$ is a —————————.

(e) This fraction shows a part of —————————. $\frac{4}{5}$

(f) This fraction shows a part of —————————. $\frac{4}{5}$

(g) In $\frac{7}{8}$, the ————————— is 7.

(h) In $\frac{9}{15}$, the ————————— is 15.

2. **Use a fraction to answer the questions below.**

(a) Three of the 5 stars were coloured. What part of the stars was coloured ?

(b) One of the 3 balloons was red. What part of the balloons was red ?

(c) Six of the 8 pencils were black. What part of the pencils was black ?

(d) Eight of the 12 pupils are boys. What part of the pupils consists of boys ?

3. **Write three equivalent fractions for each of these fractions.**

(a) $\dfrac{1}{4}$ (b) $\dfrac{1}{3}$ (c) $\dfrac{2}{5}$ (d) $\dfrac{3}{4}$ (e) $\dfrac{1}{5}$

4. **Complete.**

(a) 1 third + __ third = 2 thirds.

(b) 2 quarters + __ quarter = 3 quarters.

(c) __ eighths + 3 eighths = 5 eighths.

(d) __ sixths + 2 sixths = 5 sixths.

(e) 3 twelfths + __ twelfths = 7 twelfths.

5. **Write the fraction shown by each figure. Then change the fraction to its simplest form.**

(a)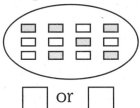

(b)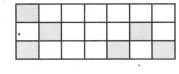

(c)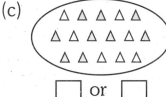

☐ or ☐   ☐ or ☐   ☐ or ☐

6. **Complete.**

(a) $\frac{1}{3}$ of 21 =   (b) $\frac{7}{8}$ of 16 =   (c) $\frac{1}{3}$ of 63 =

(d) $\frac{1}{5}$ of 100 =   (e) $\frac{3}{4}$ of 16 =   (f) $\frac{2}{5}$ of 45 =

7. (a) $3\frac{5}{6} - 1\frac{1}{3} =$ (b) $7\frac{7}{8} - 3\frac{3}{4} =$ (c) $4\frac{4}{5} - 3 =$

(d) $8\frac{1}{4} + 4\frac{3}{8} =$ (e) $9\frac{2}{3} + 5\frac{5}{6} =$ (f) $4\frac{1}{2} + 7\frac{1}{2} =$

8. How much is $\frac{1}{2}$ of 2 metres ? Give your answer in centimetres.

9. Fill in the blanks.

a. Fractions which have different denominators are called _____ fractions.

Give five examples of this type of fraction.

☐ ☐ ☐ ☐ ☐

b. A fraction whose numerator is more than its denominator is called an _____ fraction.

Give five examples of this type of fraction.

☐ ☐ ☐ ☐ ☐

c. The sum of a whole number and a proper fraction is called a _____ number.

Give five examples of this type of number.

☐ ☐ ☐ ☐ ☐

d. A fraction whose numerator is smaller than its denominator is called a _____ fraction.

Give five examples of this type of fraction.

☐ ☐ ☐ ☐ ☐

10. A bag of rice weighs $15\frac{1}{4}$ kg. A bag of sugar weighs $7\frac{3}{8}$ kg. What is their total weight ?

```
A              B
+--------------+
```

11. Measure this line AB in centimetres. How many centimetres is $\frac{1}{3}$ of AB ?

12. A boy had 25 marbles. He lost $\frac{2}{5}$ of his marbles. How many marbles did he lose ?

13. The length of one piece of string is $\frac{1}{5}$ m. What will be the total length of 4 such pieces of string ?

14. Mrs. Gupta has 4 bars of chocolate. She divides them equally among 5 boys. How much does each boy get ?

15. Sita has $3\frac{3}{4}$ m of ribbon. She uses $1\frac{3}{8}$ m of it. How much ribbon has she left ?

16. Fill in the ☐ with > , < or = .

(a) $\frac{18}{5}$ ☐ $3\frac{4}{5}$ (b) $7\frac{1}{3}$ ☐ $\frac{24}{3}$ (c) $\frac{5}{8}$ ☐ $\frac{3}{4}$

(d) $\frac{8}{2}$ ☐ 4   (e) $\frac{2}{3}$ ☐ $\frac{4}{6}$ (f) $1\frac{2}{3}$ ☐ $\frac{4}{3}$

17. Each side of a square is $\frac{3}{4}$ m long. What is the total length of all the sides of the square ?

18. Complete these.

(a) $\frac{5}{8}$ of 16 =

(b) $\frac{1}{2}$ of 16 =

(c) $\frac{1}{4}$ of 16 =

(d) $\frac{3}{4}$ of 16 =

19. One book is $\frac{3}{4}$ cm thick. What is the total thickness of 6 such books ?

20. Mary has 8 apples. She divides these equally among 6 girls. How much does each girl get ?

21. Study the figures below and write the fraction that shows the shaded part. In each case simplify the fraction.

(a)

(b)

(c)

(d)

Division of Fractions
Reciprocals

In order to understand the process of division between fractions, we must know what the term—**reciprocal**—means. The dictionary meaning of this word is **inversely correspondent** or **complementary.**

In mathematics, the reciprocal of a fraction is obtained by interchanging the positions of its numerator and its denominator ; as —

Reciprocal of $\frac{3}{4}$ is $\frac{4}{3}$ and of $\frac{2}{3}$ is $\frac{3}{2}$.

Reciprocal of $\frac{4}{5}$ is $\frac{5}{4}$ and of $\frac{5}{6}$ is $\frac{6}{5}$.

Reciprocal of $\frac{6}{11}$ is $\frac{11}{6}$ and of $\frac{7}{8}$ is $\frac{8}{7}$.

Reciprocal of 3 is $\frac{1}{3}$ $\left(\because 3 = \frac{3}{1} \right)$

Similarly, Reciprocal of 2 is $\frac{1}{2}$ and of 13 is $\frac{1}{13}$.

Remember that —

1. 1 is its own reciprocal also.
2. Two mutually reciprocal numbers when multiplied are equal to 1; as —

$$\frac{\cancel{7}}{\cancel{11}} \times \frac{\cancel{11}}{\cancel{7}} = 1 \text{ and } \cancel{5} \times \frac{1}{\cancel{5}} = 1$$

Example 1. Divide $\frac{2}{3}$ by 2.

Solution : We have to divide $\frac{2}{3}$ by 2.

Let us draw a rectangle and divide it into 3 equal parts. Now shade two of these three parts with dots.

64

Now —

Dotted part is $\frac{2}{3}$ of the rectangle.

We are to divide this part by 2.

Clearly, we shall get only **one part** as the result. This part is $\frac{1}{3}$ of the entire rectangle.

$$\therefore \frac{2}{3} \div 2 = \frac{1}{3}$$

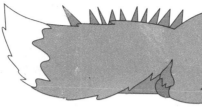

But how shall we get $\frac{1}{3}$ from $\frac{2}{3} \div 2$?

By trial we know that $\frac{2}{3} \times \frac{1}{2} = \frac{1}{3}$.

But $\frac{1}{2}$ is the reciprocal of 2.

So, we get the method for division as under :

Method :

1. Write the fraction to be divided as it is.
2. Multiply it by the reciprocal of the divisor.

Example 2. (a) Divide $\frac{2}{7}$ by 5.

(b) 5 by $\frac{10}{11}$

Solution : (a) $\frac{2}{7} \div 5 = \frac{2}{7} \times \frac{1}{5} = \frac{2}{35}$ **Ans.**

(b) $5 \div \frac{10}{11} = \frac{\overset{1}{\cancel{5}}}{1} \times \frac{11}{\underset{2}{\cancel{10}}} = \frac{11}{2} = 5\frac{1}{2}$ **Ans.**

Example 3. Divide $3\frac{1}{2}$ by $\frac{14}{15}$.

Solution : $3\frac{1}{2} \div \frac{14}{15} = \frac{7}{2} \div \frac{14}{15} = \frac{\overset{1}{7}}{2} \times \frac{15}{\underset{2}{14}} = \frac{15}{4} = \mathbf{3\frac{3}{4}}$ **Ans.**

Example 4. Divide $6\frac{3}{4}$ by $2\frac{1}{4}$.

Solution : $6\frac{3}{4} \div 2\frac{1}{4} = \frac{27}{4} \div \frac{9}{4} = \frac{\overset{3}{27}}{4} \times \frac{\cancel{4}}{\cancel{9}} = \frac{3}{1} = \mathbf{3}$ **Ans.**

Example 5. Which fraction multiplied by $6\frac{2}{3}$ will give $9\frac{3}{5}$ as product ?

Solution :

Given product $= 9\frac{3}{5} = \frac{48}{5}$

Given multiplier $= 6\frac{2}{3} = \frac{20}{3}$

$\therefore$ Multiplicand $= \frac{48}{5} \div \frac{20}{3} = \frac{\overset{12}{48}}{5} \times \frac{3}{\underset{5}{20}}$

$= \frac{36}{25} = \mathbf{1\frac{11}{25}}$ **Ans.**

Example 6. $5\frac{2}{7}$ kg of potatoes cost Rs. $10\frac{4}{7}$.

Find the cost of one kg of potatoes.

Solution : Cost of $5\frac{2}{7}$ or $\frac{37}{7}$ kg of potatoes $=$ Rs. $10\frac{4}{7} =$ Rs. $\frac{74}{7}$

For finding the cost of 1 kg, we shall have to divide the total cost by the total weight of potatoes.

$\therefore$ cost of 1 kg of potatoes $=$ Rs. $\frac{\overset{2}{74}}{7} \times \frac{7}{\underset{1}{37}} = \mathbf{Rs.\ 2}$ **Ans.**

EXERCISE I

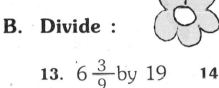

A. Divide :

1. $\frac{3}{5}$ by 4   2. $\frac{3}{4}$ by 6   3. $\frac{8}{9}$ by 4   4. $\frac{8}{17}$ by 4

5. $\frac{7}{11}$ by 14   6. $\frac{6}{11}$ by 15   7. $\frac{18}{29}$ by 9   8. $\frac{3}{7}$ by 3

9. $\frac{24}{25}$ by 12   10. $\frac{63}{65}$ by 9   11. $\frac{45}{49}$ by 15   12. $\frac{27}{29}$ by 18

B. Divide :

13. $6\frac{3}{9}$ by 19   14. $6\frac{3}{8}$ by 17   15. $7\frac{3}{5}$ by 19

16. $7\frac{4}{5}$ by 13   17. $16\frac{5}{8}$ by 19   18. $4\frac{2}{7}$ by 15

19. $9\frac{1}{3}$ by 14   20. $10\frac{1}{9}$ by 7   21. $5\frac{5}{12}$ by 26

22. $26\frac{2}{3}$ by 20   23. $15\frac{5}{8}$ by 25   24. $20\frac{5}{9}$ by 37

25. $3\frac{6}{47}$ by 49   26. $6\frac{3}{4}$ by 18   27. $5\frac{1}{3}$ by 16

28. $3\frac{3}{16}$ by 17   29. $16\frac{7}{8}$ by $5\frac{2}{5}$ 30. $18\frac{8}{9}$ by $1\frac{3}{31}$

C. Divide :

31. $\frac{5}{8}$ by $\frac{7}{10}$ 32. $\frac{9}{16}$ by $\frac{3}{8}$ 33. $\frac{2}{5}$ by $\frac{2}{3}$

34. $\frac{4}{7}$ by $\frac{8}{21}$ 35. $\frac{4}{5}$ by $\frac{8}{15}$ 36. $\frac{5}{8}$ by $\frac{15}{16}$

37. $\frac{13}{15}$ by $\frac{25}{27}$ 38. $\frac{39}{60}$ by $\frac{13}{15}$ 39. $\frac{18}{19}$ by $\frac{54}{95}$

D. Carry out these divisions :

40. $11 \div 15\frac{5}{7}$ **41.** $17 \div 6\frac{3}{8}$ **42.** $3 \div \frac{7}{11}$

43. $4 \div 15\frac{8}{9}$ **44.** $220 \div 8\frac{6}{13}$ **45.** $39 \div 5\frac{5}{12}$

46. $19 \div 16\frac{2}{7}$ **47.** $11 \div 27\frac{1}{2}$ **48.** $60 \div 13\frac{11}{13}$

49. $34 \div 6\frac{2}{11}$ **50.** $17 \div 6\frac{3}{8}$ **51.** $783 \div 15\frac{6}{17}$

E. Carry out these divisions :

52. $9\frac{4}{9} \div 8\frac{1}{2}$ **53.** $4\frac{11}{21} \div 2\frac{5}{7}$ **54.** $30\frac{3}{9} \div 5\frac{1}{10}$

55. $5\frac{5}{9} \div 1\frac{3}{7}$ **56.** $6 \div 7\frac{5}{7}$ **57.** $16\frac{7}{8} \div 1\frac{13}{32}$

58. $4\frac{6}{13} \div 7\frac{1}{4}$ **59.** $2\frac{1}{14} \div 5\frac{4}{5}$ **60.** $2\frac{1}{2} \div 3\frac{1}{3}$

61. $20\frac{5}{16} \div 1\frac{3}{13}$ **62.** $15\frac{15}{77} \div 10\frac{10}{77}$ **63.** $25\frac{4}{5} \div 4\frac{3}{10}$

64. $30\frac{3}{4} \div 10\frac{1}{4}$ **65.** $25\frac{7}{8} \div 4\frac{1}{17}$ **66.** $9\frac{7}{12} \div 3\frac{2}{7}$

67. Which fraction multiplied by $2\frac{5}{7}$ gives $4\frac{1}{14}$ as product ?

Multiplication and Division combined

Example 1. Solve : $\dfrac{2}{3} \times \dfrac{4}{5} \div \dfrac{7}{15}$

Solution : $\dfrac{2}{3} \times \dfrac{4}{5} \div \dfrac{7}{15} = \dfrac{2}{3} \times \dfrac{4}{5} \times \dfrac{15}{7}$

$$= \dfrac{2 \times 4 \times \overset{\overset{1}{5}}{\cancel{15}}}{\underset{\underset{1}{1}}{\cancel{3} \times \cancel{5}} \times 7} = \dfrac{2 \times 4}{2} = \dfrac{8}{7} = \mathbf{1\dfrac{1}{7}} \text{ Ans.}$$

Example 2. Simplify : $3\dfrac{3}{4} \div \dfrac{7}{8} \times 4\dfrac{1}{6} \div \dfrac{15}{28}$

Solution : $3\dfrac{3}{4} \div \dfrac{7}{8} \times 4\dfrac{1}{6} \div \dfrac{15}{28} = \dfrac{15}{4} \times \dfrac{8}{7} \times \dfrac{25}{6} \times \dfrac{28}{15}$

$$= \dfrac{\cancel{15} \times \overset{4}{\cancel{8}} \times 25 \times \overset{7}{\cancel{28}}}{\cancel{4} \times \cancel{7} \times \underset{3}{\cancel{6}} \times \cancel{15}} = \dfrac{25 \times 4}{2} = \dfrac{100}{3} = \mathbf{33\dfrac{1}{3}} \text{ Ans.}$$

Example 3. The product of two fractions is $3\dfrac{1}{2}$ and the reciprocal of one of the fractions is $\dfrac{4}{9}$. Find the other fraction.

Solution : Reciprocal of one fraction = $\dfrac{4}{9}$

$\therefore$ Fraction itself = $\dfrac{9}{4}$

Product of the fractions = $3\dfrac{1}{2}$ = $\dfrac{7}{2}$

Now, according to the question —

$\dfrac{9}{4} \times$ other fraction = $\dfrac{7}{2}$

$\therefore$ other fraction = $\dfrac{7}{2} \div \dfrac{9}{4}$ = $\dfrac{7}{\underset{1}{\cancel{2}}} \times \dfrac{\overset{2}{\cancel{4}}}{9} = \dfrac{14}{9} = \mathbf{1\dfrac{5}{9}}$ Ans.

EXERCISE II

A. Solve :

1. $\frac{1}{2} \div \frac{1}{2} \times \frac{1}{2}$

2. $\frac{2}{3} \times \frac{5}{6} \div 1\frac{4}{11}$

3. $\frac{1}{5} \times \frac{1}{5} \div \frac{1}{5}$

4. $\frac{2}{3} \times \frac{3}{4} \div \frac{5}{6}$

5. $\frac{2}{3} \div \frac{3}{4} \times \frac{5}{6}$

6. $\frac{1}{2} \div \frac{1}{4} \times \frac{1}{6}$

7. $\frac{3}{8} \times \frac{5}{6} \div \frac{13}{16} \div 1\frac{1}{2} \times 26$

8. $2\frac{1}{3} \div \frac{7}{16} \times 6\frac{1}{4} \div \frac{15}{28} \div 7$

9. $\left(\frac{1}{2} \div \frac{1}{2} \times \frac{1}{2} \right) \times \left(2 \div 2 \times 2 \right)$

10. $11\frac{1}{5} \times 3\frac{3}{14} \times \frac{1}{33} \div \frac{8}{17} \times 9\frac{1}{17}$

11. $6\frac{2}{3} \div 2\frac{2}{9} \times 3\frac{1}{3} \div \frac{3}{10} \times 4\frac{4}{5}$

12. $1\frac{1}{4} \div 1\frac{1}{12} \times 7\frac{4}{5} \div 1\frac{1}{2} \times 2\frac{1}{12}$

B. Simplify :

13. $\left(\frac{1}{3} \div \frac{1}{3} \times \frac{1}{3} \right) \div \left(\frac{1}{5} \div \frac{1}{5} \times \frac{1}{5} \right)$

14. $\left(\frac{1}{6} \div \frac{1}{6} \times \frac{1}{6} \right) \div \left(\frac{3}{4} \times \frac{3}{4} \div \frac{3}{4} \right)$

15. $\left(\frac{1}{2} \times \frac{1}{2} \div \frac{1}{2} \right) \div \left(\frac{1}{4} \div \frac{1}{4} \times \frac{1}{4} \right)$

16. $\left(\frac{3}{4} \div \frac{2}{3} \times \frac{5}{6} \div \frac{7}{8} \right) \div \left(2\frac{1}{4} \div \frac{1}{4} \times 5\frac{1}{5} \right)$

17. Find the fraction that on being divided by $2\frac{1}{2}$ and then multiplied by $6\frac{1}{3}$ gives $14\frac{1}{4}$ as the answer.

18. The product of two fractions is $2\frac{4}{17}$. If the reciprocal of one of the fractions be $9\frac{1}{2}$, find the other fraction.

19. A clothier bought $43\frac{3}{5}$ metres of cloth for making vests. If one vest requires $\frac{2}{5}$ metre of cloth, how many vests will be made out of the entire cloth ?

20. Which is the smaller : $\frac{8}{15} \div 5$ or $5 \div \frac{8}{15}$?

A. Tenths

Look at the number line below. It is divided into tenths.

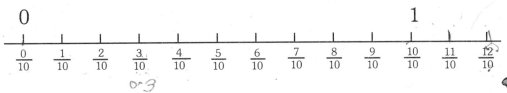

The denominators of these fractions are all 10. The fraction $\frac{1}{10}$ stands for one-tenth. The fraction $\frac{2}{10}$ stands for two-tenths. Fractions with a denominator of 10 can be written in another way.

$\frac{1}{10}$ can be written as 0.1 (zero point one).

$\frac{2}{10}$ can be written as 0.2 (zero point two).

0.1 and 0.2 are known as **decimal fractions** or **decimals**.

0.1   This is a decimal fraction.

This dot is the decimal point. The decimal point should be in a midway position as shown.

The number line and the figures below show the two ways of naming fractions.

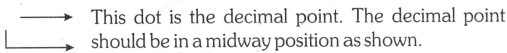

Common Name

Decimal Name

$\frac{10}{10} = 1\frac{0}{10} = 1.0$ $\frac{11}{10} = 1\frac{1}{10} = 1.1$ $\frac{12}{10} = 1\frac{2}{10} = 1.2$

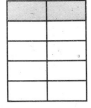 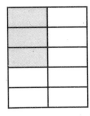 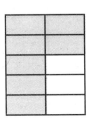 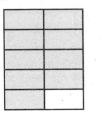 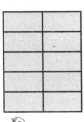

$\frac{2}{10} = 0.2$ $\frac{3}{10} = 0.3$ $\frac{7}{10} = 0.7$ $\frac{9}{10} = 0.9$ $\frac{10}{10} = 1.0$

71

Read	Common fraction form	Decimal fraction form
Three-tenths	$\frac{3}{10}$	0.3
Eight-tenths	$\frac{8}{10}$	0.8
One and two-tenths	$1\frac{2}{10}$	1.2
Five and four-tenths	$5\frac{4}{10}$	5.4
Six and zero-tenths	$6\frac{0}{10}$	6.0

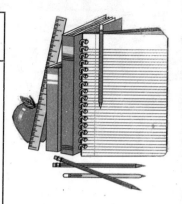

1. **Write these numbers as common fractions and as decimal fractions.**

   (a) Four-tenths   (b) Six-tenths

   (c) Two and two-tenths   (d) Three and five-tenths

   (e) Five and zero-tenths   (f) Seven and eight-tenths

Read	Common fraction form	Decimal fraction form
Ten and two-tenths	$10\frac{2}{10}$	10.2
Fourteen and five-tenths	$14\frac{5}{10}$	14.5
Twenty-one and one-tenth	$21\frac{1}{10}$	21.1
Forty-five and six-tenths	$45\frac{6}{10}$	45.6

2. **Write these numbers as common fractions and as decimal fractions.**

   (a) Ten and four-tenths   (b) Fifteen and two-tenths

   (c) Nineteen and three-tenths   (d) Twenty-three and five-tenths

   (e) Thirty-one and one-tenth   (f) Forty-four and eight-tenth

Read	Common fraction form	Decimal fraction form
6 tens, 5 units and 6 tenths	$65\frac{6}{10}$	65.6
7 units and 8 tenths	$7\frac{8}{10}$	7.8
5 tenths	$21\frac{5}{10}$	0.5

3. **Write the common fraction and the decimal fraction for each of the following :**

   (a) 8 tenths

   (b) 4 tens, 7 units and 3 tenths

   (c) 8 units and 9 tenths

   (d) 6 tens and 5 tenths

   Example :

   $$10.4 = \quad \text{1 ten, 0 units and 4 tenths}$$
   $$7.9 = \quad \text{7 units and 9 tenths}$$
   $$49.6 = \quad \text{4 tens, 9 units and 6 tenths}$$

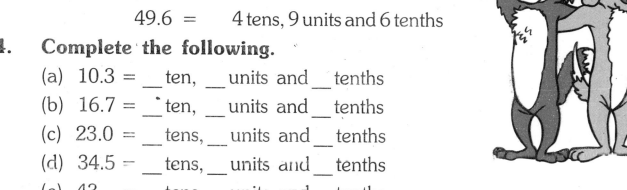

4. **Complete the following.**

   (a) 10.3 = __ ten, __ units and __ tenths

   (b) 16.7 = __ ten, __ units and __ tenths

   (c) 23.0 = __ tens, __ units and __ tenths

   (d) 34.5 = __ tens, __ units and __ tenths

   (e) 43. = __ tens, __ units and __ tenths

5. **State the common and decimal fractions shown by each set of figures.**

   a.
   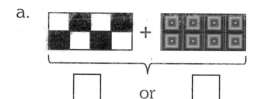
   □ or □

   b.
   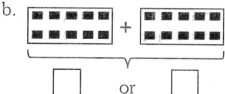
   □ or □

   c.
   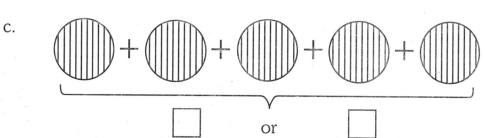
   □ or □

   d.
   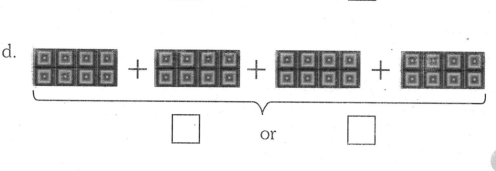
   □ or □

6. Write the following as decimal fractions.

(a) $2\frac{3}{10}$ (b) $\frac{7}{10}$ (c) $5\frac{6}{10}$ (d) $\frac{9}{10}$

(e) $8\frac{2}{10}$ (f) $4\frac{4}{10}$ (g) $7\frac{2}{10}$ (h) $9\frac{1}{10}$

(i) $10\frac{3}{10}$ (j) $14\frac{8}{10}$ (k) $18\frac{1}{10}$ (l) $23\frac{5}{10}$

7. Write the following as common fractions.

(a) 0.5 (b) 0.9 (c) 0.1 (d) 0.3

(e) 2.6 (f) 3.4 (g) 7.2 (h) 6.7

(i) 8.4 (j) 10.3 (k) 11.7 (l) 13.9

The pictures show parts of a centimetre ruler. Each centimetre is divided into 10 equal parts. Each part is $\frac{1}{10}$ or 0.1 cm.

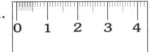 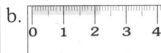 

The coloured part is $\frac{5}{10}$ cm or 0.5 cm.

The coloured part is $2\frac{2}{10}$ cm or 2.2 cm.

The coloured part is $3\frac{7}{10}$ cm or 3.7 cm.

8. Complete.

(a)

The coloured part is ☐ cm or ☐ cm.

b.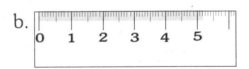

The coloured part is ☐ cm or ☐ cm.

9.

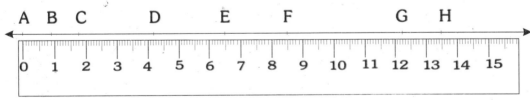

What is the length of the line AD ?

AD = $4\frac{2}{10}$ cm or 4.2 cm.

What are the lengths of the following :

(a) AB (b) AC (c) AE (d) AF (e) AG (f) AH

(g) BD (h) CF (i) FH (j) EG (k) DF (l) GH

B. Hundredths

Study the following :

1 tenth	**2 tenths**	**4 tenths**
$\frac{1}{10}$	$\frac{2}{10}$	$\frac{4}{10}$
0.1	0.2	0.4
zero point one	zero point two	zero point four

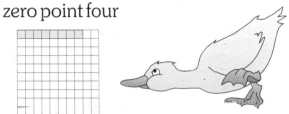

1 hundredth	**2 hundredths**	**8 hundredths**
$\frac{1}{100}$	$\frac{2}{100}$	$\frac{8}{100}$
0.01	0.02	0.08
zero point zero one	zero point zero two	zero point zero eight

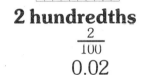

10 hundredths	**20 hundredths**	**40 hundredths**
or	**or**	**or**
1 tenth	**2 tenths**	**4 tenths**
$\frac{10}{100}$ or $\frac{1}{10}$	$\frac{20}{100}$ or $\frac{2}{10}$	$\frac{40}{100}$ or $\frac{4}{10}$
0.10 or 0.1	0.20 or 0.2	0.40 or 0.4

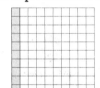 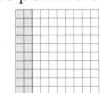 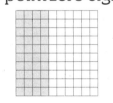 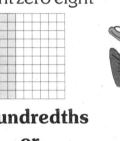

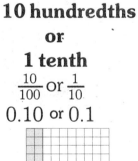 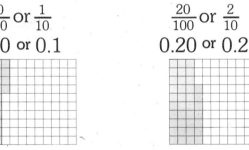 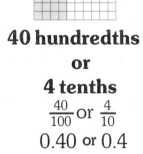 

14 hundredths	**37 hundredths**	**62 hundredths**
$\frac{14}{100}$	$\frac{37}{100}$	$\frac{62}{100}$
zero point one four	zero point three seven	zero point six two

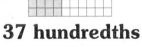 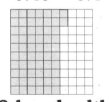  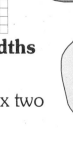

0.10 = 1tenth and 0 hundredths.

0.14 = 1tenth and 4 hundredths.

0.37 = 3tenths and 7 hundredths.

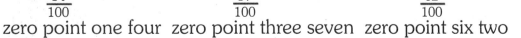 

1. **What fraction of each square is coloured ? Write this fraction in the decimal form.**

a. 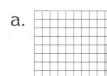 b.   c.   d.

e.   f.   g.   h.

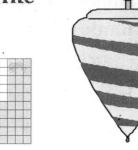

2. **Draw squares on graph paper and colour them to show :**
   (a) 0.35   (b) 0.42   (c) 0.70   (d) 0.27
   (e) 0.19   (f) 0.07   (g) 0.61   (h) 0.53

3. **Complete the following.**
   (a) $0.23 = 2$ tenths and 3 hundredths $= \frac{23}{100}$
   (b) $0.08 = \underline{\ \ }$ tenths and $\underline{\ \ }$ hundredths $=$
   (c) $0.31 = \underline{\ \ }$ tenths and $\underline{\ \ }$ hundredth $=$
   (d) $0.50 = \underline{\ \ }$ tenths and $\underline{\ \ }$ hundredths $=$
   (e) $0.65 = \underline{\ \ }$ tenths and $\underline{\ \ }$ hundredths $=$
   (f) $0.72 = \underline{\ \ }$ tenths and $\underline{\ \ }$ hundredths $=$
   (g) $0.84 = \underline{\ \ }$ tenths and $\underline{\ \ }$ hundredths $=$
   (h) $0.96 = \underline{\ \ }$ tenths and $\underline{\ \ }$ hundredths $=$

4. **Write as decimals.**

(a) $\frac{15}{100}$ (b) $\frac{9}{100}$ (c) $\frac{8}{100}$ (d) $\frac{27}{100}$

(e) $1\frac{30}{100}$ (f) $1\frac{31}{100}$ (g) $1\frac{62}{100}$ (h) $1\frac{29}{100}$

(i) $2\frac{53}{100}$ (j) $2\frac{60}{100}$ (k) $3\frac{75}{100}$ (l) $3\frac{88}{100}$

(m) $2\frac{8}{100}$ (n) $3\frac{80}{100}$ (o) $2\frac{51}{100}$ (p) $3\frac{45}{100}$

5. Fill in the ☐ with >, < or =.

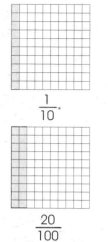

$\frac{1}{10}$

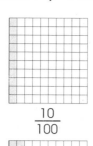

$\frac{10}{100}$

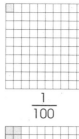

$\frac{1}{100}$

$\frac{19}{100}$

$\frac{20}{100}$

$\frac{2}{10}$

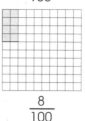

$\frac{8}{100}$

$\frac{21}{100}$

(a) 0.01 ☐ 0.1   (b) $\frac{1}{10}$ ☐ $\frac{10}{100}$ (c) 0.08 ☐ 0.1

(d) 0.21 ☐ 0.2   (e) $\frac{2}{10}$ ☐ $\frac{10}{100}$ (f) $\frac{20}{100}$ ☐ 0.2

(g) 0.19 ☐ 0.2   (h) $\frac{21}{100}$ ☐ $\frac{2}{10}$ (i) $\frac{19}{100}$ ☐ $\frac{21}{100}$

Place value of digits before the decimal point	Place value of digits after the decimal point
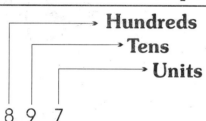 Hundreds → Tens → Units	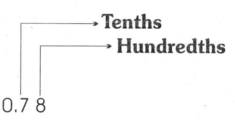 Tenths → Hundredths
8 9 7	0.7 8
8 stands for 8 hundreds or 800	7 stands for seven -tenths or 0.7
9 stands for 9 tens or 90	8 stands for eight-hundredths or 0.08.
7 stands for seven units or 7	

What is the place value of each digit in 576.48 ?

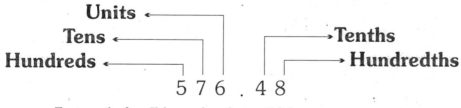

Units ← Tens ← Hundreds ← Tenths → Hundredths →

5 7 6 . 4 8

5 stands for 5 hundreds or 500.

7 stands for 7 tens or 70.

6 stands for 6 units or 6

4 stands for 4 tenths or $\frac{4}{10}$ or 0.4

8 stands for 8 hundredths or $\frac{8}{100}$ or 0.08

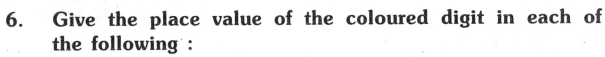

0.48 may be read as 4 tenths and 8 hundredths
or 48 hundredths.

0.94 may be read as 9 tenths and 4 hundredths
or 94 hundredths.

6. **Give the place value of the coloured digit in each of the following :**

(a) 5.7**6**   (b) 8**3**.11   (c) 91.**3**9   (d) 9**7**3.91

(C) Thousandths

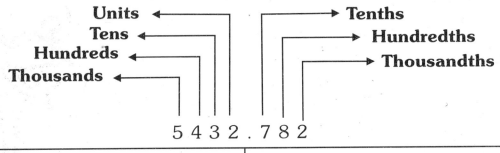

Units ← → Tenths
Tens ← → Hundredths
Hundreds ← → Thousandths
Thousands ←

5 4 3 2 . 7 8 2

Place value of digits before the decimal point	Place value of digits after the decimal point
The 5 in the thousand's place stands for 5000.	The 7 in the tenth's place means $\frac{7}{10}$ or 0.7.
The 4 in the hundred's place stands for 400.	The 8 in the hundredth's place means $\frac{8}{10}$ or 0.08.
The 3 in the ten's place stands for 30.	The 2 in the thousandth's place means $\frac{2}{1000}$ or 0.002.
The 2 in the unit's place stands for 2.	

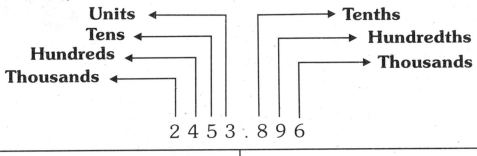

Units ← → Tenths
Tens ← → Hundredths
Hundreds ← → Thousands
Thousands ←

2 4 5 3 . 8 9 6

Place value of digits before the decimal point	Place value of digits after the decimal point
2 stands for 2 thousands or 2000	8 stands for 8 tenths or $\frac{8}{10}$ or 0.8.
4 stands for 4 hundreds or 400	9 stands for 9 hundredths or $\frac{9}{100}$ 0.09.
5 stands for 5 tens or 50	
3 stands for 3 units or 3	6 stands for 6 thousandths or $\frac{6}{1000}$ or 0.006.

1. **Give the place value of the digit 5 in each of the following.**

   (a) 1364.512
   (b) 1573.498
   (c) 2472.651
   (d) 5146.873
   (e) 7625.139
   (f) 4196.235

2. **Complete the following.**
   (a) 236.64 The 4 in the hundredth's place means $\frac{4}{100}$
   (b) 156.72 The 7 in the _____ place means ____
   (c) 439.28 The 3 in the _____ place means ____
   (d) 561.48 The 5 in the _____ place means ____
   (e) 12.689 The 9 in the _____ place means ____
   (f) 7652.3 The 7 in the _____ place means ____

   0.345   may be read as
            3 tenths, 4 hundredths and 5 thousandths or
            3 tenths and 45 thousandths or
            34 hundredths and 5 thousandths
            or 345 thousandths.

3. **Write the following as decimals.**
   (a) 2 tenths, 5 hundredths and 4 thousandths.
   (b) 5 tenths, 3 hundredths and 6 thousandths.
   (c) 8 tenths, and 43 thousandths.
   (d) 4 tenths and 11 thousandths.
   (e) 3 tenths, 0 hundredths and 9 thousandths.
   (f) 6 tenths and 8 thousandths.
   (g) 273 thousandths.
   (h) 607 thousandths.
   (i) 53 hundredths and 2 thousandths.
   (j) 86 hundredths and 1 thousandth.
   (k) 1 tenth, 8 hundredths and 8 thousandths.
   (l) 7 tenths and 70 thousandths.

D. Tenths, hundredths and thousandths

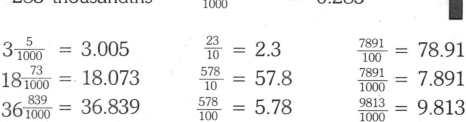

5 tenths	$=$	$\frac{5}{10}$	$=$	0.5
5 hundredths	$=$	$\frac{5}{100}$	$=$	0.05
5 thousandths	$=$	$\frac{5}{1000}$	$=$	0.005
85 thousandths	$=$	$\frac{85}{1000}$	$=$	0.085
285 thousandths	$=$	$\frac{285}{1000}$	$=$	0.285

$3\frac{5}{1000} = 3.005$ $\qquad \frac{23}{10} = 2.3$ $\qquad \frac{7891}{100} = 78.91$

$18\frac{73}{1000} = 18.073$ $\qquad \frac{578}{10} = 57.8$ $\qquad \frac{7891}{1000} = 7.891$

$36\frac{839}{1000} = 36.839$ $\qquad \frac{578}{100} = 5.78$ $\qquad \frac{9813}{1000} = 9.813$

Write the following as decimals.

1. (a) $\frac{3}{100}$ (b) $\frac{6}{10}$ (c) $\frac{9}{1000}$ (d) $\frac{8}{100}$
2. (a) $\frac{7}{1000}$ (b) $\frac{15}{100}$ (c) $\frac{36}{1000}$ (d) $\frac{18}{10}$
3. (a) $\frac{27}{100}$ (b) $\frac{35}{10}$ (c) $\frac{15}{1000}$ (d) $2\frac{7}{10}$
4. (a) $\frac{45}{100}$ (b) $\frac{98}{1000}$ (c) $\frac{70}{100}$ (d) $\frac{70}{1000}$
5. (a) $3\frac{8}{10}$ (b) $\frac{112}{100}$ (c) $\frac{342}{100}$ (d) $1\frac{25}{100}$
6. (a) $\frac{345}{100}$ (b) $\frac{112}{10}$ (c) $\frac{2123}{1000}$ (d) $1\frac{367}{1000}$
7. (a) $15\frac{75}{100}$ (b) $12\frac{3}{10}$ (c) $\frac{4218}{1000}$ (d) $\frac{5251}{100}$
8. (a) $15\frac{8}{10}$ (b) $12\frac{86}{100}$ (c) $15\frac{742}{1000}$ (d) $\frac{9219}{1000}$

We can write decimals as mixed numbers like this :

$\qquad 3.56 = 3\frac{56}{100} \qquad 25.7 = 25\frac{7}{10}$

Now write these as mixed numbers.

9. (a) 2.72 (b) 27.2 (c) 10.7 (d) 1.07
10. (a) 3.56 (b) 35.6 (c) 45.63 (d) 45.63
11. (a) 17.92 (b) 1.792 (c) 5.525 (d) 55.25
12. (a) 157.8 (b) 15.78 (c) 15.78 (d) 18.06
13. (a) 18.06 (b) 1.806 (c) 25.56 (d) 255.6
14. (a) 25.56 (b) 27.45 (c) 2.743 (d) 274.3
15. (a) 5.31 (b) 27.68 (c) 2.476 (d) 600.5
16. (a) 7.413 (b) 250.7 (c) 1.125 (d) 7.425

17. Complete the following.

(a) $\frac{3}{10}$, $\frac{4}{10}$, ___, ___, $\frac{7}{10}$, ___, ___, ___, $\frac{11}{10}$.

(b) 0.8, 0.9, 1.0, ___, ___, ___, ___, 1.5 .

(c) $\frac{8}{100}$, $\frac{9}{100}$, ___, ___, ___, ___, $\frac{14}{100}$.

(d) 0.28, 0.29, ___, ___, ___, 0.33, ___, ___ .

(e) 0.04, 0.05, ___, ___, 0.08, ___, ___, ___ .

(f) 2 tenths, 4 tenths, __,__,__, 12 tenths.

(g) 6 hundredths, __, 10 hundredths, 12 hundredths, __ .

(h) 0.48, 0.50, 0.52, __, __, __, __ .

(i) 0.123, 0.126, 0.129, __,__,__,__ .

(j) $\frac{45}{100}$, $\frac{50}{100}$, $\frac{55}{100}$, __, __, __, __ .

(k) $\frac{22}{1000}$, $\frac{24}{1000}$, $\frac{26}{1000}$, __, __, __, __ .

(l) 3.3, —, 3.9, __, __, __, __ .

(m) 1.85, __, 1.95, __, __, __, __ .

(n) 3.676, __, 3.696, __, __, __, __ .

18. Write these numbers in order of size, putting the smallest first.

(a) 0.35, 0.53, 0.3

(b) 0.84, 0.48, 0.4

(c) 0.52, 0.2, 0.25

(d) 0.96, 0.9, 0.69

(e) 0.7, 0.97, 0.79

(f) 0.98, 0.9, 0.89

(g) 1.26, 1.62, 1.2

(h) 3.54, 3.45, 3.5

19. Write these numbers in order of size, putting the largest first.

(a) 0.003, 0.3, 0.03

(b) 0.08, 0.008, 0.8

(c) 0.016, 0.16, 1.6

(d) 0.021, 2.21, 0.21

(e) 0.425, 4.25, 42.5

(f) 6.31, 0.631, 63.1

(g) 0.123, 0.231, 0.321

(h) 0.689, 0.986, 0.698

E. Fractions and decimals

This figure is divided into 100 small squares.
35 out of the 100 squares are coloured.

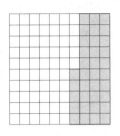

$$\frac{35}{100} = \frac{3}{10} + \frac{5}{100} = 0.35$$

$$0.35 = 3 \text{ tenths} + 5 \text{ hundredths}$$

Look at this :

$$\frac{659}{1000} = \frac{6}{10} + \frac{5}{10} + \frac{9}{1000} = 0.659$$

$$0.659 = 6 \text{ tenths} + 5 \text{ hundredths} + 9 \text{ thousandths}$$

1. Write the following as decimals.

(a) $\frac{2}{10} + \frac{5}{100}$ (b) $\frac{4}{10} + \frac{8}{100}$ (c) $\frac{1}{10} + \frac{4}{100}$

(d) $\frac{3}{10} + \frac{7}{100}$ (e) $\frac{9}{10} + \frac{1}{100}$ (f) $\frac{6}{10} + \frac{3}{100}$

(g) $\frac{2}{10} + \frac{4}{100} + \frac{6}{1000}$ (h) $\frac{5}{10} + \frac{3}{100} + \frac{7}{1000}$ (i) $\frac{1}{10} + \frac{9}{100} + \frac{6}{1000}$

(j) $\frac{6}{10} + \frac{8}{100} + \frac{7}{1000}$ (k) $\frac{6}{10} + \frac{6}{100} + \frac{6}{1000}$ (l) $\frac{7}{10} + \frac{3}{100} + \frac{1}{1000}$

We can write a decimal as a sum of a series of fractions like this :

$$0.432 = \frac{4}{10} + \frac{3}{100} + \frac{2}{1000}$$

2. Now do these in the same way.

(a) 0.15   (b) 0.37   (c) 0.68   (d) 0.91

(e) 0.215   (f) 0.369   (9) 0.485   (h) 0.307

(i) 0.567   (j) 0.798   (k) 0.922   (l) 0.864

3. Write the following as decimals.

(a) $1 + \frac{3}{10} + \frac{5}{100}$ (b) $1 + \frac{7}{10} + \frac{4}{400}$

(c) $1 + \frac{8}{10} + \frac{2}{100}$ (d) $2 + \frac{5}{10} + \frac{9}{100}$

(e) $2 + \frac{6}{10} + \frac{3}{100}$ (f) $3 + \frac{8}{10} + \frac{6}{100}$

(g) $1 + \frac{2}{10} + \frac{4}{100} + \frac{5}{1000}$ (h) $1 + \frac{9}{10} + \frac{6}{100} + \frac{3}{1000}$

(i) $2 + \frac{9}{10} + \frac{5}{100} + \frac{7}{1000}$ (j) $3 + \frac{7}{10} + \frac{4}{100} + \frac{9}{1000}$

F. **Express simple common fractions as decimals**

A common fraction can be renamed as an equivalent fraction whose denominator is 10 or 100. It can then be changed into a decimal fraction.

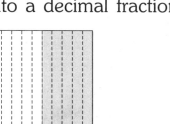

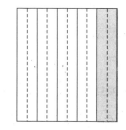

$\frac{1}{2} = \frac{1 \times 5}{2 \times 5} = \frac{5}{10} = 0.5$ $\frac{1}{5} = \frac{1 \times 2}{5 \times 2} = \frac{2}{10} = 0.2$

It is easy to change fractions having 2, 4, 5 and 20 as their denominators into decimal fractions.

(1) Write $2\frac{1}{4}$ as a decimal.   **(2)** Write $3\frac{3}{20}$ as a decimal.

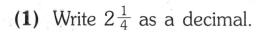

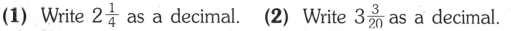

$\frac{1}{4} = \frac{1 \times 25}{4 \times 25} = \frac{25}{100} = 0.25$ $\frac{3}{20} = \frac{3 \times 5}{20 \times 5} = \frac{15}{100} = 0.15$

$2\frac{1}{4} = 2.25$ $3\frac{3}{20} = 3.15$

1. **Change the following to tenths or hundredths and then write as decimals.**

(a) $\frac{2}{5}$ (b) $\frac{3}{5}$ (c) $\frac{1}{2}$ (d) $\frac{1}{5}$

(e) $\frac{3}{5}$ (f) $\frac{1}{20}$ (g) $\frac{7}{20}$ (h) $\frac{17}{20}$

2. **Write the following as decimals.**

(a) $1\frac{1}{2}$ (b) $2\frac{1}{4}$ (c) $3\frac{1}{5}$ (d) $1\frac{3}{4}$

(e) $2\frac{2}{5}$ (f) $4\frac{3}{5}$ (g) $1\frac{7}{20}$ (h) $3\frac{1}{5}$

(i) $3\frac{9}{20}$ (j) $3\frac{13}{20}$ (k) $8\frac{3}{5}$ (l) $7\frac{3}{4}$

(m) $4\frac{3}{4}$ (n) $2\frac{11}{20}$ (o) $4\frac{11}{20}$ (p) $9\frac{4}{5}$

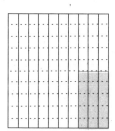

83

G. **Express decimals as fractions**

Look at these :

(1) $1.6 = 1\frac{6}{10} = 1+\frac{6}{10} = 1+\frac{6\div2}{10\div2}$
$= 1+\frac{3}{5} = 1+\frac{3}{5}$

(2) $2.25 = 2\frac{25}{100} = 2+\frac{25}{100} = 2+\frac{25\div25}{100\div25}$
$= 2+\frac{1}{4} = 2\frac{1}{4}$

Write the following as fractions in their simplest forms.

1. (a) 2.8	(b) 0.9	(c) 3.3	(d) 0.7
2. (a) 0.8	(b) 1.1	(c) 5.4	(d) 6.5
3. (a) 0.25	(b) 3.75	(c) 2.80	(d) 7.35
4. (a) 0.65	(b) 4.05	(c) 7.5	(d) 8.45

H. **Exercises on fractions**

1. Draw a line 9.5 cm long.

2. Colour 0.37 of figure **(a)**, 0.3 of figure **(b)**, 0.78 of figure **(c)** and 0.03 of figure **(d)**.

(a) 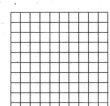 (b) 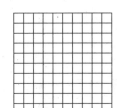 (c) 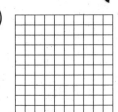 (d)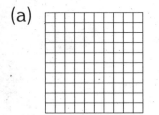

3. **Complete the following.**

Common fractions	Decimals
$\frac{1}{10}$	
$\frac{4}{1000}$	
	0.3
$\frac{10}{10}$	

Common fractions	Decimals
	0.001
$\frac{7}{20}$	
	0.25
$\frac{100}{100}$	

ADDITION AND SUBTRACTION OF DECIMAL FRACTIONS

I. Addition of decimal fractions

Look at this picture :

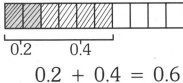

0.2 + 0.4 = 0.6

$$\begin{array}{r} 0.2 \\ +\ 0.4 \\ \hline 0.6 \end{array}$$

1. Now do these.

(a) 0.1+0.5 =   (b) 0.3+0.4 =   (c) 0.2+0.7 =

(d) $\begin{array}{r} 0.3 \\ +0.3 \\ \hline \end{array}$ (e) $\begin{array}{r} 0.2 \\ +0.6 \\ \hline \end{array}$ (f) $\begin{array}{r} 0.4 \\ +0.5 \\ \hline \end{array}$ (g) $\begin{array}{r} 0.6 \\ +0.1 \\ \hline \end{array}$

(h) 0.2+0.3+0.4   =   (i) 0.1+0.5+0.2 =

Look at this :

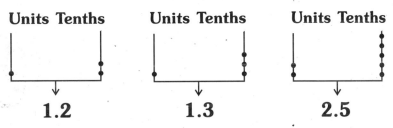

1.2   **1.3**   **2.5**

We can write the addition in two ways.

(1) 1.2+1.3 = 2.5

(2) $\begin{array}{r} 1.2 \\ +\ 1.3 \\ \hline 2.5 \end{array}$

2. Complete each picture and write the addition in two ways.

(a)
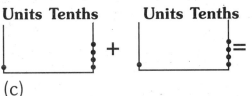

(b)
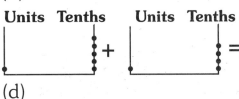

(c)   (d)
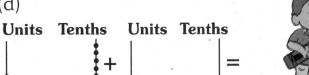

85

Addition on the number line

Look at this number line :

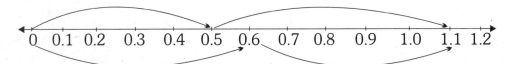

This number line shows $0.5 + 0.6 = 1.1$ and $0.6 + 0.5 = 1.1$

3. Write down what these number lines show.

a.
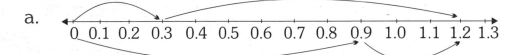

b.
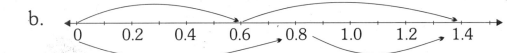

c.
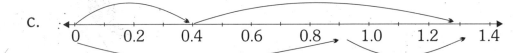

d.
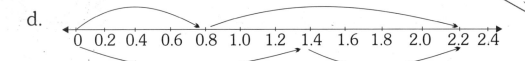

e.
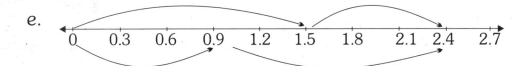

f.
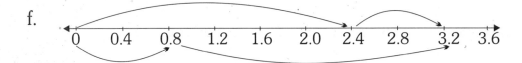

4. Add.

  (a) 0.5+0.8   (b) 1.5+0·9   (c) 0.6+1.8

  (d) 1.4+0.9   (e) 0.3+1·8   (f) 0.7+1·5

  (g) 1.5+1.6+1.2 (h) 0.6+1.7+14 (i) 1.1+0.7+0.5

  (j) 2.1+1.9+10.8 (k) 2.6+1.5+1.8 (l) 1.9+0.9+1.7

J. Subtraction of decimal fractions
Subtraction on the number line
Look at this number line :

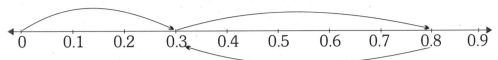

This number line shows 0.3+0.5 = 0.8 and 0.8 —0.5 = 0.3.

1. Write down what these number lines show.

a.
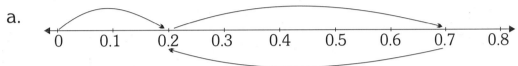

b.
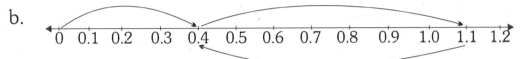

c.
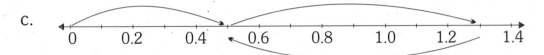

d.
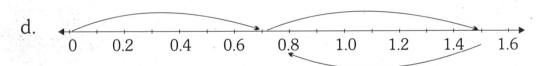

e.
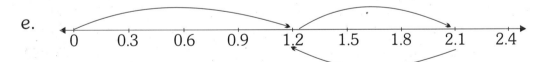

f.
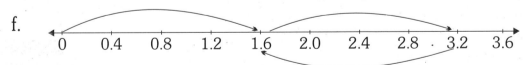

2. Subtract.

(a) 1.8—0.3 (b) 2.6—0.4   (c) 2.9—0.7

(d) 1.5—0.9 (e) 2.1—0.3 (f) 2.3—0.6

(g) 5.1—1.5 (h) 4.2—2.7 (i) 6.5—3.8

(j) 7.0—5.6 (k) 4.6—2.9 (1) 6.4—3.6

K. Further addition

T e n s	U n i t s	.	T e n t h s	H u n d r e d t h s
2	6	.	8	7
1	2	.	5	9
3	9	.	4	6

↑
decimal points

Explanation

Step 1 : 7 hundredths+9 hundredths
= 16 hundredths
= 1 tenth and 6 hundredths.
Write 6 in the hundredth's place.

Step 2 : 8 tenths+5 tenths+1 tenth
= 14 tenths
= 1 unit and 4 tenths.
Write 4 in the tenth's place.

Step 3 : 6 units+2 units+1 unit=9 units
Write 9 in the unit's place.

Step 4 : 2 tens+1 ten= 3 tens.
Write 3 in the ten's place.

The decimal points of the numbers to be added must be directly below one another. Then add in the usual way. The decimal point in the answer must also be directly below the other decimal points.

Add.

1. (a) 13.56   (b) 21.73   (c) 26.57   (d) 34.93
       +15.77   +13.49   +24.84   +23.78

2. (a)   4.61   (b)   2.09   (c)   8.57   (d) 18.57
       + 2.58   + 3.17   + 6.25   + 10.08

3. (a) 15.36   (b) 18.51   (c) 23.54   (d) 39.07
         13.24   21.73   27.43   21.50
       +11.53   +16.58   +12.68   +13.88

4. (a) 23.74   (b) 41.81   (c) 34.56   (d) 48.96
         18.56   27.08   10.09   22.59
       +29.70   +13.07   +25.54   +13.75

L. Further subtraction

Tens	Units	.	Tenths	Hundredths
3	$^4\cancel{5}$	.	$^1\cancel{^12}$	^{16}
−1	3	.	5	7
2	1	.	6	9

↑
decimal points

Explanation

Step 1 : 2 tenths
= 1 tenth + 10 hundredths.
16 hundredths —7 hundredths
= 9 hundredths.
Write 9 in the hundredth's place.

Step 2 : 5 units
= 4 units + 10 tenths.
11 tenths—5 tenths = 6 tenths.
Write 6 in the tenth's place.

Step 3 : 4 units — 3 units = 1 unit
Write 1 in the unit's place.

Step 4 : 3 tens — 1 ten = 2 tens.
Write 2 in the ten's place.

The decimal points of the numbers to be subtracted must be directly below one another. Then subtract in the usual way. The decimal point in the answer must be directly below the other points.

Subtract.

1. (a) 26.17
      −13.59

   (b) 31.45
      −15.68

   (c) 30.03
      −14.65

   (d) 32.85
      −16.29

2. (a) 45.05
      −18.76

   (b) 38.50
      −19.87

   (c) 41.06
      −12.84

   (d) 48.40
      −23.65

3. (a) 51.54
      −28.78

   (b) 58.21
      −33.49

   (c) 62.54
      −47.86

   (d) 75.01
      −32.72

4. (a) 13.03
      − 5.76

   (b) 21.16
      −15.08

   (c) 30.50
      −17.75

   (d) 36.72
      −27.79

89

M. Further exercises on addition and subtraction

Fill in the missing numbers.

Working

(1) ☐ +18.78 = 42.6

    23.82+18.78 = 42.6

$$\begin{array}{r} 42.60 \\ -18.78 \\ \hline 23.82 \end{array}$$

(2) ☐ − 8.9 = 23.76

    32.66−8.9 = 23.76

$$\begin{array}{r} 8.90 \\ +23.76 \\ \hline 32.66 \end{array}$$

(3) 26.73− ☐ = 4.9

    26.73−21.83 = 4.9

$$\begin{array}{r} 26.73 \\ -4.90 \\ \hline 21.83 \end{array}$$

1. **Write these sums in the vertical form and then add them. (Make sure the decimal points are below one another.)**

(a) 3.5+2.6+4.2

(b) 13.5+8.6+24.5

(c) 25.2+21.4+18.9

(d) 32.5+0.05+13.81

(e) 13.49+24.75+10.05

(f) 34.8+18.25+17.02

(g) 12.14+6.57+13.46

(h) 7.73+13.08+15.77

(i) 21.54+13.68+17.63

(j) 19.01+4.58+2191

(k) 5.33+21.75+30.5

(l) 17.36+40.51+13.09

2. **Write these sums in the vertical form and subtract them.**

(a) 35.0—25.25

(b) 38.12—27-75

(c) 41.56—37.77

(d) 45.06—36.59

(e) 55.51—38.74

(f) 60.14—37.57

(g) 18.1—9.62

(h) 20.0—6.34

(i) 28.91—13.97

(j) 33.04—27.59

(k) 44.23—12.76

(l) 54.71—36.84

3. **Fill in the missing numbers.**

(a) ☐ +7.9 = 18.31

(b) 9.01— ☐ = 0.06

(c) 17.3— ☐ = 8.78

(d) ☐ —4.38 = 3.2

(e) ☐ +4.32 =7.06

(f) 8.78+ ☐ = 10.7

(g) 5.2+ ☐ = 13.32

(h) 7.3+ ☐ = 9.06

(i) 18.4— ☐ = 0.83

(j) ☐ —5-3 = 8.99

(k) 7.36+ ☐ = 13.5

(l) 19.76— ☐ = 8.5

N. Word problems

(a) A bag of rice weighs 7.6 kg. A bag of sugar weighs 2.5 kg. How much heavier is the bag of rice ?

		Working
A bag of rice weighs	7.60 kg	7.60 kg
A bag of sugar weighs	2.25 kg	−2.25 kg
The bag of rice is heavier by	5.35 kg	5.35 kg

(b) Mrs. Gupta bought 16.25 metres of red ribbon and 4.5 metres of black ribbon. How much ribbon did she buy altogether ?

			Working
Mrs. Gupta bought	16.25 m	of red ribbon.	16.25 m
and	4.50 m	of black ribbon.	+4.50 m
Altogether she bought	20.75 m	of ribbon.	20.75 m

Do these.

1. Find the total length of the sides of the triangle ABC.

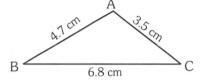

2. A piece of wire is 20.5 metres long. It is cut into two pieces. If one piece is 7.75 metres long, what is the length of the other piece ?

3. The length of rectangle ABCD is 4.3 cm and its width is 2.9 cm.

   (a) What is the perimeter of ABCD.

   (b) What is the difference in length between AB and BC ?

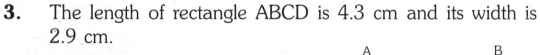

4. Measure the lengths of pencil A and pencil B.

   (a) What is the total length of both the pencils ?

   (b) What is the difference in their lengths ?

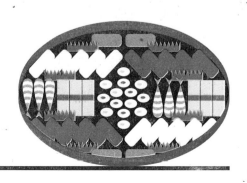

5. Priya bought a pencil case for Rs 2.85 and a pen for Rs 4.05. How much did she spend altogether ?

6. Mrs. Kapoor bought a book for Rs 77.95. She gave the sales-girl Rs 100.00. How much change did she receive ?

7. Mrs. Rahman bought $5\frac{1}{4}$g kg of rice and $2\frac{1}{2}$ kg of sugar. How much rice and sugar did she buy altogether ? Give your answer in decimals.

8. Mary bought a box of chocolates for Rs 66.65. She gave the shopkeeper 70.00. How much change did she receive?

9. Akash is 1.25 metres tall. His brother is 0.3 metres taller. How tall is his brother ?

10. A woman bought 4.25 metres of brown cloth and 3.65 metres of blue cloth. How much cloth did she buy ?

11. A boy has three pieces of ribbon. One piece is 3.98 metres long, another is 5.76 metres and the third is 10.57 metres. What is the total length of the three pieces of string ?

12. Mohan measures 1.69 metres. Reeta is 0.49 metres shorter than Mohan. What is Reeta's height ?

13. A baby weighed 2.95 kg when she was born. After 6 months she weighed 5.90 kg. How much weight did she gain ?

14. A bunch of grapes weighs 1.13 kilograms. A second bunch of grapes weighs 0.98 kilograms. (a) What is the total weight of the two bunches of grapes ? (b) What is the difference in their weights ?

15. A piece of string 17.5 m long is cut into two pieces. One piece is 8.96 m long. What is the length of the other piece ?

16. Mary bought $1\frac{1}{2}$ kg of potatoes and $1\frac{3}{4}$ kg of flour. How much flour and potatoes did she buy altogether ? Give your answer in decimals.

17. John weighs 36.5 kg. His brother is heavier by 3.7 kg. What is his brother's weight ?

9 GRAPHS

Column graphs on squared paper

1. The table below shows the number of cars sold by a company in the first 6 months of the year.

January	February	March	April	May	June
12	18	12	24	30	24

We can use a picture graph to show this :

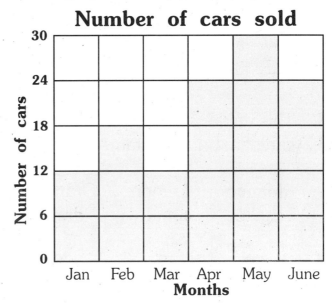

Number of cars sold

represents 6 cars

January   February   March   April   May   June

We can also show this by making a column graph on squared paper.

We write the months along the horizontal axis and the number of cars along the vertical axis. Another name for a column graph is **histogram**.

(a) In which month were most cars sold ?

(b) In which months were least cars sold ?

(c) What was the difference between the number of sales in January and that in May ?

(d) In which months was the sale twice that in January ?

(e) What was the total number of cars sold in the first 6 months ?

2. This column graph shows the time taken by each of the five teams to complete a piece of work.

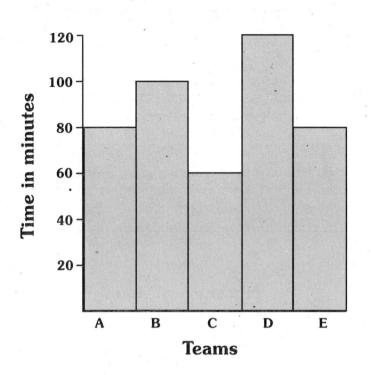

(a) Which team completed the work in the shortest time ?

(b) Which team took the longest time ?

(c) Which teams took the same length of time ?

(d) What was the shortest time taken ?

(e) How long did team B take ?

(f) Which team took half the time taken by team D ?

(g) How many hours did team D take ?

(h) What was the total time taken by the five teams ?

3. This table shows the marks scored by seven pupils in a test.

Sanjay	Anil	Dillip	Kailash	Ramesh	Naresh	Aman
50	85	55	60	70	40	50

Draw a column graph to show these marks. Write four sentences about your graph.

4. This table shows the number of bottles of six kinds of drinks sold in the canteen on a certain day.

Mango shake	Lemon drink	Orange drink	Sugar-cane drink	Milk	Chocolate milk
60	48	72	24	12	36

Draw a column graph to show the number of bottles of drinks sold. Write four sentences about your graph.

5. This column graph shows the number of litres of petrol used by a taxi during a week.

(a) How many litres of petrol were used on Monday ?

(b) On which days was most petrol used ?

(c) On which days was least petrol used ?

(d) On which days was the amount of petrol used three times that used on Sunday ?

(e) What was the difference in the amount of petrol used on Saturday and Sunday ?

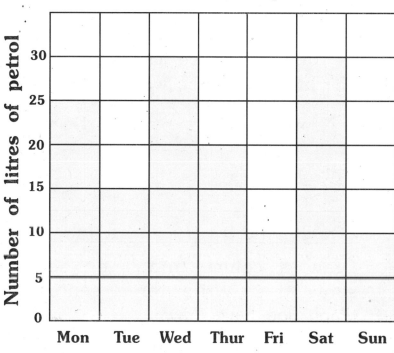

Number of litres of petrol used

Y-axis: Number of litres of petrol (0, 5, 10, 15, 20, 25, 30)

X-axis: Mon, Tue, Wed, Thur, Fri, Sat, Sun — **Days of the week**

(f) Find the total amount of petrol used for the week and divide it by 7. This gives the average number of litres of petrol used for each day of the week.

(g) On which days was the amount used below the average ?

6. The table shows the distances some pupils travel to school.

Names	Reeta	Priya	Poonam	Renu	Alok	Ashok	Anuj
Distances in kilometres	3.5	2.5	6.0	5.5	2.5	5.0	4.5

Draw a column graph on squared paper to show this. Write three sentences about the graph you have drawn.

7. (a) Ask a pupil to measure your height, using a tape measure and write the answer in centimetres.

(b) Make a table showing your height and the heights and names of six other pupils in your class.

(c) Use squared paper to make a graph from the table you have just made.

8. The table shows the weights of six pupils.

Names	Dillip	Sonu	Deepak	Raman	Anuj	Sunil
Weights in kilograms	24	36	30	24	30	24

Draw a column graph on squared paper to show this. Write three sentences about the graph you have drawn.

9. Make a table of shoe sizes and the number of pupils who wear each size in your class.

Use squared paper to make a column graph from your table.

Use your column graph to answer the following :

(a) What shoe size do most pupils in your class wear ?

(b) What shoe size do the least number of pupils in your class wear ?

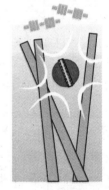

10. Find out the games the pupils in your class play. Draw a table showing the games and the number of pupils who play such games. Use squared paper to make a column graph from your table.

Use your column graph to answer the following :

(a) Which game is the most popular in your class ?

(b) Which game is the least popular in your class ?

10 CIRCLES

A. Parts of a circle

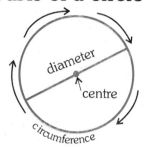 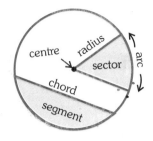 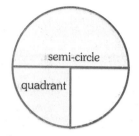

A **circle** is the path traced out by a point moving at a fixed distance from a given fixed point called the **centre.** We can also describe a circle as a flat shape formed by a set of points at an equal distance from a fixed point.

The perimeter of a circle is called the **circumference.** A part of the circumference is called an **arc.** A straight line joining two points on the circumference is called a **chord.**

The **diameter** is the longest chord that passes through the centre of the circle. The distance from the centre to the circumference is the **radius.** The radius of any circle is half its diameter.

A circle may be divided into 2 halves. A half-circle is called a **semi-circle.** If a circle is divided into quarters, each quarter-circle is called a **quadrant.**

B. Construction of circles

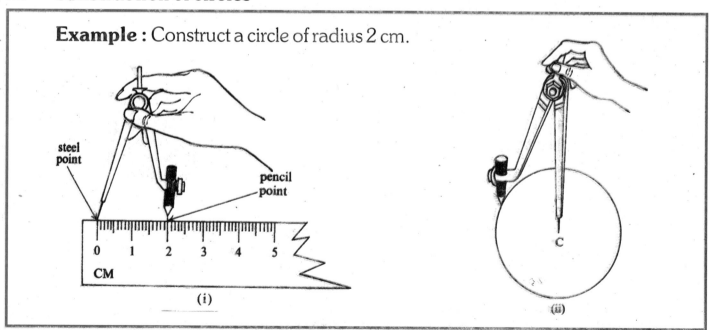

Example : Construct a circle of radius 2 cm.

1. Open the legs of the compasses to the required radius length of 2 cm.
2. Mark a point on your piece of paper for the centre of the circle.
3. Place the steel point of the compasses at this mark and move the pencil point along the paper to trace out the circle.
4. The drawn circle has a radius of 2 cm.

1. Draw circles with the following radii.

    (a)   2.5 cm   (b) 3 cm   (c)   4.5 cm   (d) 1.5 cm

2. Draw circles with the following diameters.

    (a)   4.4 cm   (b) 2 cm   (c)   5 cm   (d) 3.2 cm

3. Draw a circle of radius 2 cm. Using the same centre draw another circle of radius 3.5 cm. What is the diameter of the smaller circle ? What is the diameter of the bigger circle ?

C. Circumference of a circle

The **circumference** of any circle is a little more than 3 times its diameter.

The ratio $\dfrac{\text{circumference}}{\text{diameter}}$ is given a special sign π (pronounced 'pie'). π is a Greek letter.

Accurate measurements show that π is approximately 3.14 or $\dfrac{22}{7}$.

Therefore, $\dfrac{\text{circumference}}{\text{diameter}} = \pi$

    or circumference $= \pi \times$ diameter

             $= \pi \times 2r$

             $= 2\pi r$, where r is the radius.

We can find the circumference of any circle if we know its radius or diameter.

$$\boxed{\text{Circumference of circle} = 2\pi r}$$

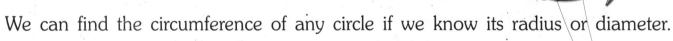

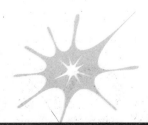

Example 1 : The radius of a circle is 5 cm. Find its circumference.

(Take π = 3.14)

$$\text{Circumference of circle} = 2\pi r$$
$$= 2 \times 3.14 \times 5 \text{ cm}$$
$$= 31.4 \text{ cm}$$

Example 2 : The circumference of a circle is 33 cm. Find its radius.

(Take $\pi = \frac{22}{7}$)

$$\text{Radius} = \frac{\text{Circumference}}{2\pi}$$
$$= \frac{33}{2 \times \frac{22}{7}} \text{ cm}$$
$$= \frac{\overset{3}{\cancel{33}}}{2} \times \frac{7}{\underset{2}{\cancel{22}}} \text{ cm}$$
$$= \frac{21}{4} \text{ cm}$$
$$= 5\frac{1}{4} \text{ cm}$$

1. Taking $\pi = \frac{22}{7}$, find the circumference of a circle of radius :
   (a)   70 cm   (b)   35 cm   (c)   28 cm   (d)   14 cm

2. Taking π = 3.14, find the circumference of a circle of diameter :
   (a)   42 cm   (b)   9 cm   (c)   19.8 cm   (d)   11.2 cm

3. Taking π = 3.14, find the circumference of a circle with circumference :
   (a)   6.28 cm   (b)   15.7 cm   (c)   25.12 cm   (d)   56.52 cm

4. The diameter of a long-playing record is 30 cm. Find its circumference.

(Take π = 3.14)

5. What is the circumference of a circular pond whose diameter is 35 m ?

(Take $\pi = \frac{22}{7}$)

Example 3 :   The diameter of a bicycle wheel is 28 cm. Find its circumference. What distance is covered in 100 revolutions ?

$$\text{Circumference of wheel} = \pi \times \text{diameter}$$
$$= \frac{22}{\cancel{7}_{1}} \times \overset{4}{\cancel{28}}$$
$$= 88 \text{ cm}$$

Distance covered in 1 revolution = circumference of wheel.

∴   Distance covered in 100 revolutions = 100 × 88 cm
$$= 8800 \text{ cm}$$
$$= 88 \text{ m}$$

6. A bicycle wheel has a radius of 28 cm. What distance does it cover in three complete turns ?

7. The radius of a wheel is 37.52 cm. Find the distance it covers when it completes 1 revolution. How many metres does it cover in 100 revolutions ?

8. Draw a circle with the help of compasses. Name its centre as O. Draw
    (a)   A radius OP.
    (b)   A diameter AB.
    (c)   A chord PQ.
    (d)   An arc RS.
    (e)   A semi-circle ATB.

9. How many chords of a circle can we draw ? Choose the correct answer.
    (a)   2   (b) 3   (c)   4
    (d)   any number.

10. Fill in the blanks to make each of the following statements true :
    (a)   Of all the chords of a circle, a diameter is the ———— chord.
    (b)   The length of all radii of a circle is ———— .
    (c)   The centre of a circle always lies on its ———— .
    (d)   There are ———— semi-circles of a circle.
    (e)   If we join any two points on a circle, we get a ———— .

11. Identify objects from your environment which can be used to draw a circle.

12. Draw a circle with radius 3 cm. Draw in it three chords of lengths 2 cm, 3.5 cm and 5 cm. respectively.

D. Area of a circle

Activity 1 : Take a piece of 1-cm square paper and draw on it circles of radii 2 cm, 3 cm, 4 cm and 5 cm. Divide the cm squares into $\frac{1}{2}$ cm squares for more accurate estimation of the area of each circle. Count the number of small squares inside each circle. If more than half a square is inside the circle, count it as a whole square. Ignore a small square if less than half of it is inside the circle.

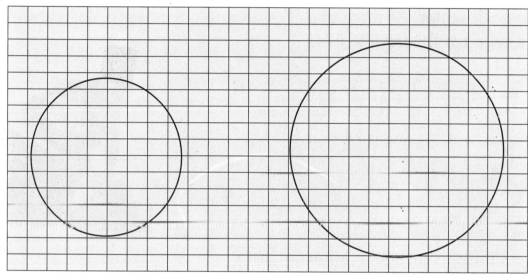

Record your estimation in the form of a table as shown below.

Radius of circle	Number of squares	Area of circle	Square of radius	$\dfrac{\text{Area of circle}}{\text{Square of radius}}$
2 cm	52 half-cm squares	$\frac{88}{7}$ cm²	4 cm	$\frac{88}{7} \times \frac{1}{4} = \frac{88}{28} = \frac{44}{14} = \frac{22}{7}$
3 cm				
4 cm				
5 cm				

What do you notice about the ratio of the area of the circle to the square of its radius ? Are all the values nearly the same ?

If you have worked carefully you will find that in each case the area of the circle is a little more than 3 times the square of its radius.

Activity 2: Draw a circle of radius 5 cm on a piece of drawing paper. Draw a diameter AB. Place a protractor with its centre at the centre of the circle and mark out angles at intervals of 15° until you reach 180°. At each 15° mark, draw a diameter.

Your circle should look like the one shown. You have divided the angle at the centre of the circle into 24 equal parts. You have therefore divided the area of the circle into 24 equal parts. Each part is called a **sector.**

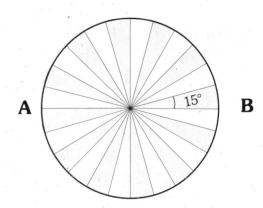

Carefully cut out each sector. Arrange and paste the sectors on a cardboard like this.

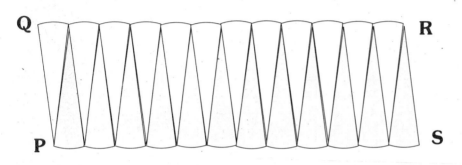

The new shape PQRS is roughly a rectangle.

(a) What can you say about the length of this rectangle and the circumference of the circle ? Is PS about half the circumference?

(b) What can you say about the breadth of this rectangle and the radius of the circle ? Is RS about the same as the radius of the circle ?

(c) Since area of rectangle PQRS = PS x RS, this activity shows that

$$\text{area of circle} = \text{PS} \times \text{RS}$$
$$= \tfrac{1}{2}\ \text{circumference}\ \times\ \text{radius}$$

But circumference of circle = $2\pi r$, where r is the radius.

Therefore area of circle $= \tfrac{1}{2} \times 2\pi r \times r$
$= \pi r^2$

$$\text{Area of circle} = \pi\ \text{radius}^2$$

Example 1 : Find the area of a circle of radius 10 cm. (Take $\pi = 3.14$)

Radius, r = 10 cm
Area of circle $= \pi r^2$
$= (3.14 \times 10^2)\ \text{cm}^2$
$= 314\ \text{cm}^2$

Example 2 : The area of a circle is 154 cm². What is its diameter ?

$$\pi r^2 = 154 \text{ cm}^2 \qquad \qquad \left(\text{Take } \pi = \frac{22}{7}\right)$$

$$\frac{22}{7} \times r^2 = 154$$

$$r^2 = 154 \times \frac{7}{22}$$

$$= 7 \times 7$$

$$\therefore r = \sqrt{7 \times 7} = 7$$

$$\therefore \text{Diameter} = 2 \times 7 \text{ cm} = 14 \text{ cm}$$

1. Taking $\pi = 3.14$, find the areas of these circles :
   (a) radius = 5 cm
   (b) radius = 8 cm
   (c) diameter = *12* m
   (d) radius = 2.5 m
   (e) diameter = 1.2 m
   (f) diameter = 2.4 m

2. Taking $\pi = \frac{22}{7}$, find the areas of these circles :
   (a) radius = 14 cm
   (b) diameter = 7 m
   (c) diameter = 21cm

3. Taking $\pi = \frac{22}{7}$, find the diameters of the circles whose areas are :

   (a) 616 cm²
   (b) $50\frac{2}{7}$ cm²
   (c) 1.54 m²
   (d) 38.5 m²

4. The radius of a circular tray is 10.5 cm. Find its area.

5. A circular pond is 42 metres across at its widest point. What is its area ?

6. Find the area of a quadrant if the radius is 7 cm. (A quadrant is a quarter of a circle.)

7. In this figure, the diameter of the big circle is 20 cm and that of the smaller circle is 14 cm. Find the area of the shaded region. Take $\pi = \frac{22}{7}$.

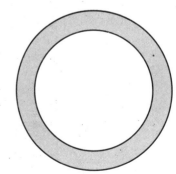

8. Find the area of a semi-circle if the radius is 7 cm.

9. The area of a circle is 154 cm². What is its circumference.

10. The diameters of the three circles in this figure are 21 cm, 14 cm and 7 cm. What is the area of the coloured region ?

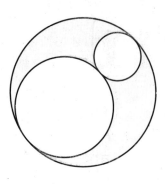

11. The circumference of the circle is 132 cm. A quadrant is cut off from the circle. Find the area of the quadrant.

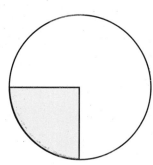

12. The distance round a circular pool is 88 m. What is the area of the pool ?

13. Solve these clues to the word puzzle.

(a) Part of the circumference.

(b) The longest straight line possible in a circle.

(c) Straight line from centre to circumference.

(d) Formed by two radii and an arc.

(e) Wheels are this shape.

(f) Perimeter of a circle.

(g) Formed by an arc and a chord.

(a)							C							
(b)							I							
(c)							R							
(d)							C							
(e)							L							
(f)							E							
(g)							S							

11 ANGLES

A. The Angle

An **angle** is actually an amount of turning or rotation. We can represent an angle by using two line segments such as AB and BC. BC is fixed while AB rotates about point B, forming the angle ABC (shown by the coloured region). Angle ABC can be written ∠ABC. Sometimes we use small letters like a, b, c, or x, y, z to represent angles. The point B in the figure is called the **vertex.**

AB and **BC** are the **arms** of the angle.

1. Name all the angles you can find in the following figures.

(a)
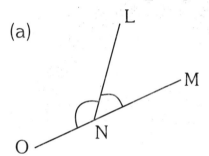

(b)
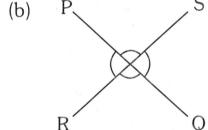

(c)
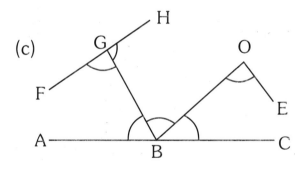

(d)
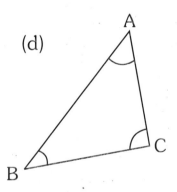

2.

Fill in the blanks.

(a) ∠ EAB = ―――

(b) ∠ ABC = ―――

(c) ――――― = c°

(d) ――――― = d°

B. The protractor

We use a **protractor** to measure or draw an angle. The size of an angle is measured in **degrees**.

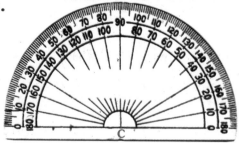

Look at the picture of the protractor. It has 2 semi-circular scales, each starting at 0° and ending at 180°. The straight line at the base from which the scales start and end is called the **base line.** C is the centre of the protractor.

C. Measurement of angles

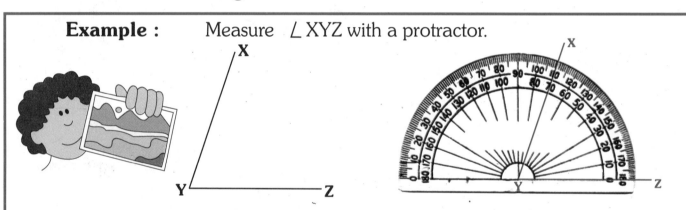

Example :   Measure ∠XYZ with a protractor.

1. Place the centre of the protractor on the point Y, and adjust the protractor so that its base line lies exactly along the line YZ. In other words, YZ must pass through the 0° mark.

2. Since the line XY passes through the 70° mark, the angle XYZ is equal to 70°.

NOTE :   If necessary, the lines YX and YZ may be projected so that they pass through the protractor marks.

1. Use a protractor to measure the following angles.

(a)

∠A B C = ____

(b)

∠P Q R = ____

(c)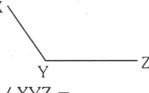

∠ XYZ = ———

(d)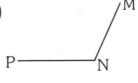

∠ MNP = ———

(e)

∠ X= ———

(f)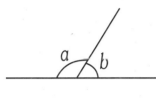

∠a=———
∠b=———
∠c=———
∠d=———

2. Measure the angles using a protractor and complete the statements.

(a)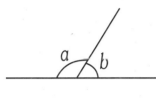

∠a=———
∠b=———
∠a+ ∠b=———

(b)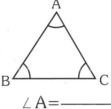

∠ A=———
∠ B=———
∠ C=———
∠A+ ∠B+ ∠C=———

(c)

∠a=———
∠b=———
∠c=———
∠d=———
∠a+ ∠b+ ∠c+ ∠d = ———

D. Construction of angles

Example : Draw an angle of 75 .

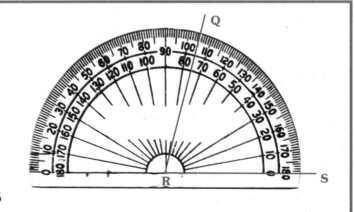

R ——————— S

1. Draw a straight line RS.
2. Place the centre of the protractor on the point R and adjust the protractor so that the line RS passes through the 0° mark.
3. Make a mark at the point where the scale shows 75° (point Q).
4. Remove the protractor and draw a line from R to Q.
5. The angle SRQ is 75°.

With a ruler and a protractor, draw the following angles.

(a) 60°   (b) 90°   (c) 120°   (d) 48°   (e) 135°   (f) 52°

E. Types of angles according to size

Some angles are given special names because of their size.
An angle less than 90° is called an **acute** angle.

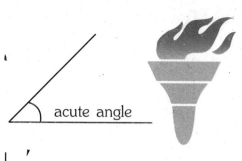

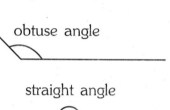

A 90° angle is called a **right** angle.

An angle greater than 90° but less than 180 is called an **obtuse** angle.

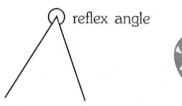

An angle of 180° is called a **straight** angle.

An angle greater than 180° but less than 360° is called a **reflex** angle.

1. Name each of the following angles, and measure its size using a protractor.

(a)

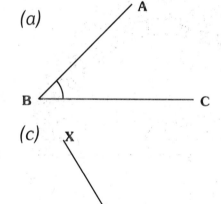

(b)

(c)

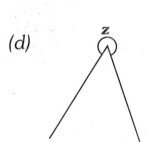

(d)

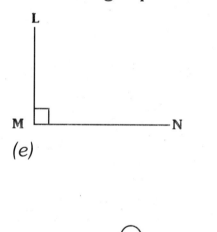

(e)

2. Draw the following angles using a ruler and a protractor and say whether they are acute, obtuse, reflex or right angles.
   (a) 50°   (b) 200°   (c) 94°   (d) 89°   (e) 90°

F. Types of angles according to position

Some angles are given special names because of their positions.

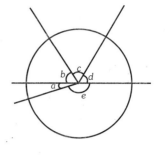

(a) When two or more angles have the same vertex, they are known as **angles at a point.**
Angles a, b, c, d and e are all angles at a point.

$$\angle a + \angle b + \angle c + \angle d + \angle e = 360°$$
$$= \text{one complete turn.}$$

The angles at a point always add up to 360°.

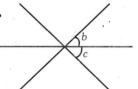

(b) When two angles at a point have one arm in common and lie on opposite sides of that arm, they are known as **adjacent angles.**
Angles b and c are adjacent angles.

(c) When two adjacent angles add up to 180°, they are known as **supplementary angles.**

Angles c and d are supplementary because LM is a straight line. $\angle c + \angle d = 180°$

Angles c and d are also known as **angles on a straight line.**

(d) When two adjacent angles add up to 90°, they are known as **complementary angles.**

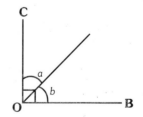

Angles a and b are complementary because $\angle COB$ is a right angle. $\angle a + \angle b = 90°$

(e) When two (or more) straight lines cross each other forming four (or more) angles at a point, then the pairs of angles opposite to each other are known as **vertically opposite angles.**

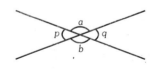

$$\text{angle } a = \text{angle } b$$
$$\text{angle } p = \text{angle } q$$

Vertically opposite angles are always equal to each other.

1. Identify the following angles.

(a)
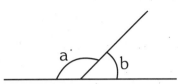

(b)
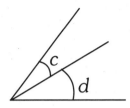

(c)
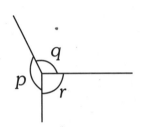

(d)
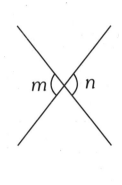

(e)
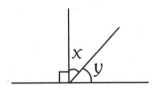

(f)
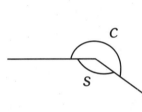

2. Fill in the blanks. All the lines in the figures are straight lines.

(a)
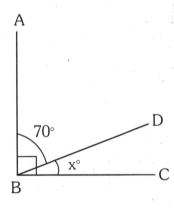

$\angle ABD + \angle DBC = 90^{0}$ (complementary angles)

$\therefore 70° + x° = 90°$

$x° =$ _____

(b)
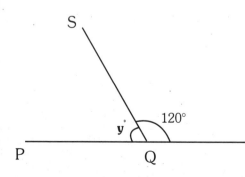

$\angle SQP + \angle SQR = 180°$ (supplementary angles)

$y° + 120° = 180°$

$y° =$ _____

12 TRIANGLES

A. Construction of triangles

We can draw triangles using ruler and compases only if all the 3 sides are given.

Example 1 : Draw a triangle ABC such that AB = 6 cm, BC = 5 cm and AC = 4 cm.

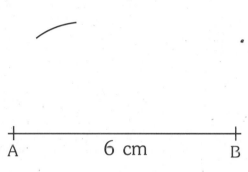 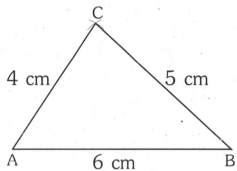

1. Draw a line AB of length 6 cm.
2. With A as centre and a radius of 5 cm, draw an arc above AB.
3. With A as centre and a radius of 4 cm, draw another arc to cut the first arc at C.
4. Join BC and AC.
5. The required triangle is triangle ABC.

1. Draw a triangle PQR such that PQ = 5 cm, PR = 6 cm and QR = 3 cm.

2. Draw a triangle with sides 3 cm, 4 cm and 5 cm. What kind of triangle is this ?

3. Draw a triangle with all its sides equal to 6 cm. What kind of triangle is this ?

4. Draw a triangle ABC such that BC = 7 cm and AB = AC = 6 cm. What kind of triangle is this ?

5. Draw a triangle XYZ such that XY = 6.5 cm, YZ = 4.8 cm and XZ = 5 cm. Measure the size of each angle.

Example 2 :   Draw a triangle PQR such that PQ = 5 cm, PR = 3.5 cm and
∠ RPQ = 60°.

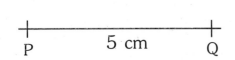

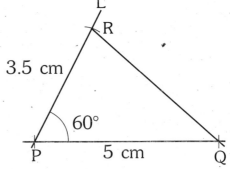

1.   Draw a straight line PQ of length 5 cm.
2.   Construct an angle of 60° at P.
3.   Mark off a point R on PL such that PR = 3.5 cm.
4.   Join RQ.
5.   PQR is the required triangle.

Example 3 :   Draw a triangle XYZ such that XY = 4.5 cm, ∠ ZXY = 70° and
∠XYZ = 35°.

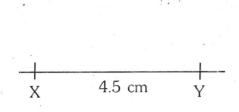

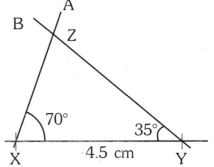

1.   Draw a straight line XY of lenght 4.5 cm.
2.   Use your protractor to make off an angle of 70° at X.
3.   Use your protractor to mark off an angle of 35° at Y.
4.   Let XA and YB meet at Z.
5.   ZYZ is the required triangle.

6.   Using ruler and compasses only, draw a triangle ABC such that AB = 7 cm,
AC = 4 cm and   CAB = 45°.

7.   Using ruler and compasses only, draw a triangle XYZ such that YZ = 6.5 cm,
∠ XYZ = 30° and and ∠ YZX = 60°.

8.   Draw an isosceles triangle JKL such that JK = JL = 5.5 cm and ∠ LJK = 130°.
Measure KL.

B. Types of triangles according to sides

A **triangle** is a three-sided closed figure. Triangles can be grouped according to the lengths of their sides.

(a) **Scalene triangles**
Look at these 3 triangles.

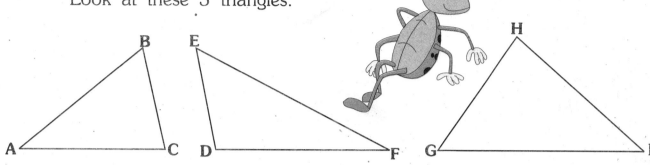

Measure the sides of each triangle and complete the table.

Triangle ABC	AB = _____ cm	BC = _____ cm	AC = _____ cm
Triangle DEF	DE = _____ cm	EF = _____ cm	DF = _____ cm
Triangle GHI	GH= _____ cm	HI = _____ cm	GI = _____ cm

Are the sides of triangle ABC equal ?
Are the sides of triangle DEF equal ?
Are the sides of triangle GHI equal ?

A triangle with all its sides unequal in length is called a **scalene** triangle.

Measure the angles. Are they all different in size ?

Draw 4 scalene triangles. Name each triangle and measure the sides.

(b) **Isosceles triangles**
Look at these 3 triangles.

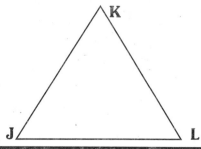
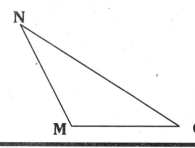
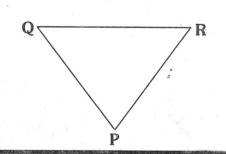

Measure the sides of each triangle and complete the table.

Triangle JKL	JK = _____ cm	KL = _____ cm	JL = _____ cm
Triangle MNO	MN = _____ cm	NO = _____ cm	MO = _____ cm
Triangle PQR	PQ = _____ cm	QR = _____ cm	PR = _____ cm

Which sides of triangle JKL are equal ?
Which sides of triangle MNO are equal ?
Which sides of triangle PQR are equal ?

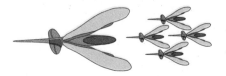

A triangle with any two sides equal in length is called an **isosceles** triangle.
Measure the angles. **Remember that the angles opposite the two equal sides are also equal.**

Draw 4 isosceles triangles. Name each triangle and measure the sides.

(c) **Equilateral triangles**
Look at these 2 triangles.

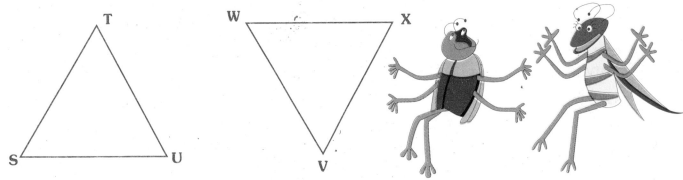

Measure the sides of each triangle and complete the table :

Triangle STU	ST = _____ cm	TU = _____ cm	SU = _____ cm
Triangle VWX	VW = _____ cm	WX = _____ cm	VX = _____ cm

Is ST = TU = SU ?
Is VW = WX = VX ?

A triangle with all its three sides equal in length is called an **equilateral** triangle.
Measure the angles. In an equilateral triangle, all three angles are also equal. Each angle is equal to 60°.

Draw 4 equilateral triangles. Name each triangle and measure the sides.

Activity 1 : Take a rectangular piece of paper and fold it down the middle. Join the two corners by a straight line. Cut along this line and open out. You now have three triangles.

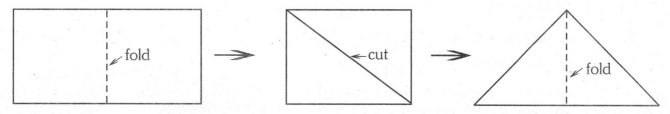

(a) Measure the sides of the largest triangle. How many sides are equal ?

(b) What name do you give to the largest triangle ?

(c) Measure the angles of the largest triangle. How many angles are equal ?

(d) Is the fold the axis of symmetry of the isosceles triangle ?

(e) Trace out the isosceles triangle in your exercise book and mark the equal sides, equal angles and the axis of symmetry.

Activity 2 : Collect three ice-cream sticks of equal length and make a hole at each end. Join the ends with paper fasteners. Hold the triangle you have formed firmly on a page of your exercise book. Draw round the inner edge.

(a) What name do you give to this triangle ?
(b) Measure the angles. Are they all equal ? What is each angle ?

(c) Draw the equilateral triangle on a piece of paper. Cut it out. Find the lines of symmetry by folding. How many lines of symmetry are there in an equilateral triangle ?

   1. Look at these triangles. Without measuring the sides, can you tell which are scalene triangles, isosceles triangles and equilateral triangles ?

Measure the sides of each triangle to check if your guess is correct.

2. **Name the following triangles :**
   (a) All the sides of the triangle are equal.
   (b) Two of the three sides of the triangle are equal.
   (c) All the sides of the triangle are unequal.

3. **Is it possible to draw a right-angled triangle with**
   (a) all the three sides equal ?
   (b) two of the three sides equal ?
   (c) all the three sides unequal ?
   Draw them, if you can.

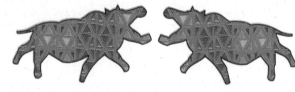

4. **Draw a triangle ABC in which AB = AC = 5 cm and ∠ A = 60°.**
   (a) Measure the third side of the triangle.
   (b) What kind of triangle is ABC ? ·
   (c) Draw the perpendicular bisector of AB.
   (d) Does the perpendicular bisector pass through C ?
   (e) What is the angle between this bisector and the side AC ?

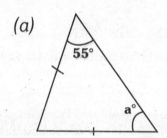

5. **Draw a triangle PQR in which PQ = 6 cm, ∠P = 50° and ∠Q = 80°.**
   (a) Measure the side QR.
   (b) What kind of triangle is PQR ?
   (c) Draw the perpendicular bisector of PR.
   (d) Does the perpendicular bisector pass through Q ?
   (e) What is the angle between this bisector and the side PQ ?

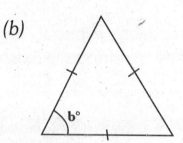

6. **In each of these triangles, find the size of the angles marked by small letters.**

(a)   *(b)*   *(c)*

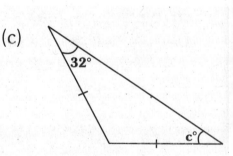

C. Types of triangles according to angles
   Triangles are also grouped according to the size of their angles.
   (a) An **acute-angled** triangle has all
        its angles less than 90°.
        ∠a, ∠b and ∠c are all acute,
        i.e. less than 90°.

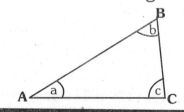

(b) **An obtuse-angled** triangle has one angle more than 90°.

∠m is obtuse, i.e. more than 90°.

∠1 and ∠3 are acute.

(c) **A right-angled** triangle has one angle equal to 90°.

∠y = 90°.

XZ is called the **hypotenuse.**

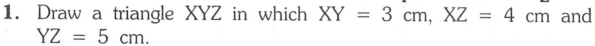

1. Draw a triangle XYZ in which XY = 3 cm, XZ = 4 cm and YZ = 5 cm.

   (a) Measure the angle X.

   (b) What kind of triangle is XYZ ?

   (c) Does this triangle have a line of symmetry ?

2. Draw a triangle EFG in which EG = 7cm, and ∠E= ∠G= 30°.

   (a) Measure the third angle of the triangle.

   (b) Is EFG an acute-angled or obtuse-angled triangle ?

   (c) Measure the sides EF and FG.

3. Draw a triangle JKL in which KL = 6.5 cm, and ∠K= ∠L= 45°.

   (a) Measure the angle J.

   (b) Measure the sides JK and JL.

D. **Angles of a triangle**

A triangle has 3 angles. Let us find out about the sum of the 3 angles of a triangle.

Activity 1: Place three pieces of paper one on top of the other. Draw a triangle on the top piece of paper. Cut along the sides of this triangle. You will get three triangles of the same size. Mark the vertices of the triangles.

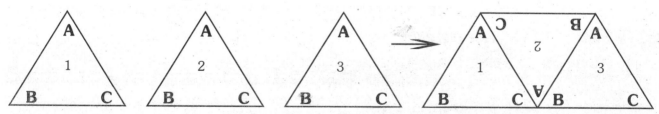

Arrange the three triangles together as shown in the diagram. You have learnt that a straight angle is an angle that contains 2 right angles or 180°. What can you say about the sum of the 3 angles of a triangle ?

Activity 2 : Draw a triangle on a piece of paper and cut it out. Mark the 3 angles of the triangle. Tear off the corners and arrange them as shown.

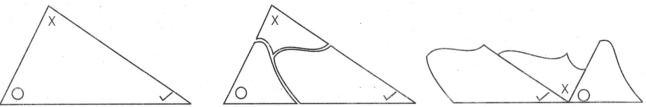

What do you notice about the sum of the angles of the triangle ?

Activity 3: Cut out a triangle ABC from a piece of paper. Mark the middle points of AB and BC and fold it as shown in (i) so that B lies on the side AC. Now fold along the dotted line as shown in (ii) so that A is at B. Finally fold along the dotted line as shown in (iii) so that C is at B. What can you say about the sum of the angles of the triangle ?

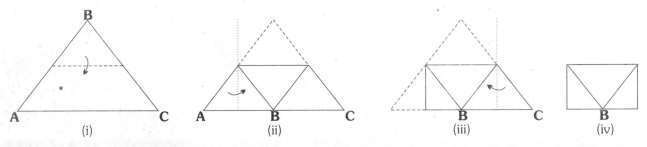

The sum of the angles in a triangle is equal to 180 degrees or a straight angle.

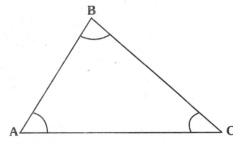

The sum of the angles in a triangle is equal to 180 degrees or 2 right angles.
180 degrees is written as 180°.
In triangle ABC,
$\angle BAC + \angle ABC + \angle ACB = 180°$.

E. Sides of a triangle

Activity : Take three pieces of rods (which can be of different or same lengths). Form a triangle with these rods. Mark the sides of the triangle as a, b and c as shown in (i).

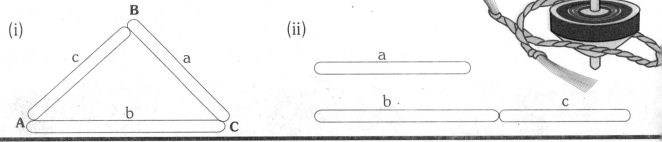

(a) Compare the length of side *a* with the sum of the lengths of sides *b* and *c* by placing the rods as shown in (ii). Is the sum of the lengths of sides *b* and *c* greater than or less than the length of side *a* ?

(b) Compare the length of side *b* with the sum of the lengths of sides *a* and *c*. Which is greater, *b* or *a+c* ?

(c) Compare the length of side *c* with the sum of the lengths of sides *a* and *b*. Which is less, *c* or *a+b* ?

The sum of the lengths of any two sides of a triangle is greater than the length of the third side.

1. **In each of these triangles, find the size of the angles marked by small letters. (Do not measure the angles.)**

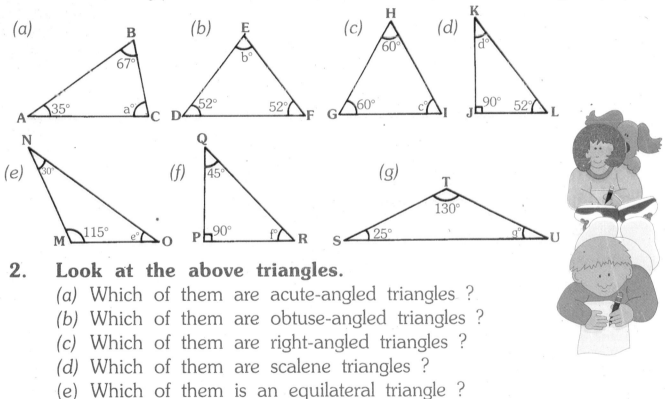

2. **Look at the above triangles.**
   (a) Which of them are acute-angled triangles ?
   (b) Which of them are obtuse-angled triangles ?
   (c) Which of them are right-angled triangles ?
   (d) Which of them are scalene triangles ?
   (e) Which of them is an equilateral triangle ?
   (f) Which of them are isosceles triangles ?

3. **Complete these sentences.**
   (a) An equilateral triangle has _____ lines of symmetry.
   (b) An equilateral triangle has _____ sides equal.
   (c) Each angle of an equilateral triangle is _____ .
   (d) An isosceles triangle has _____ lines of symmetry.
   (e) An isosceles triangle has _____ sides equal.
   (f) An isosceles triangle has _____ angles equal.

Use this figure to answer questions 4.8.

AB = BC
AC = AE
CE = AE
AF = EF
∠ABC = 90°
∠CDE = 90°
∠AFE = 120°
∠ECD = 25°

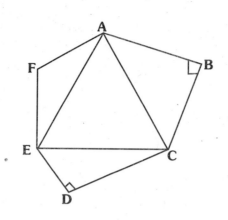

4. **Name :**
   (a) the isosceles triangles
   (b) the equilateral triangle
   (c) the isosceles but not equilateral triangles
   (d) the right-angled triangle
   (e) the right-angled and isosceles triangle

5. **In triangle ABC, find the size of the base angles.**
6. **In triangle ACE, what is the size of each angle ?**
7. **In triangle AEF, find the size of the base angles.**
8. **In triangle ECD, find the size of ∠DEC.**
9. **Draw an isosceles triangle ABC with sides AB = BC = 6 cm and AC = 8 cm.**
   (a) Which are the equal angles ?
   (b) Measure an equal angle.
   (c) Without measuring, find the third angle of the triangle.

10. **Draw a triangle PQR with sides PQ = 7 cm, PR = 6 cm and ∠RPQ = 53°.**
    (a) What type of triangle is triangle PQR ?
    (b) Measure ∠QRP.
    (c) Without measuring, find the third angle of the triangle.

11. **Draw three triangles of different sizes.**
    (a) Measure the largest angle of each triangle.
    (b) Measure the shortest side of each triangle.

12. The picture below shows three triangles. Measure the angles and sides of each triangle and complete the tables.

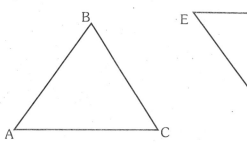
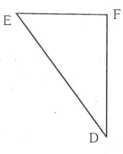
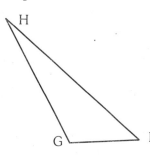

∠A =	BC =	∠D =	EF =	∠G =	HI =
∠B =	AC =	∠E =	DF =	∠H =	GI =
∠C =	AB =	∠F =	DE =	∠I =	GH =

(a) In each triangle, name the largest angle and the longest side.

(b) Is the largest angle opposite the longest side of each triangle ?

(c) In each triangle, name the smallest angle and the shortest side.

(d) Is the smallest angle opposite the shortest side of each triangle ?

F. Interior and exterior angles of triangles

Suppose we have an angle ABC. We know that B is its vertex and BA and BC are its arms. Now the space inside the arms BA and BC is called the **interior** of ∠ABC and so ∠1 is the **interior angle.**

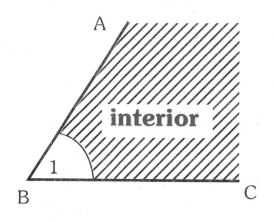

But the space outside the arms BA and BC forms the exterior of ∠ABC and so ∠2 is called the exterior angle.

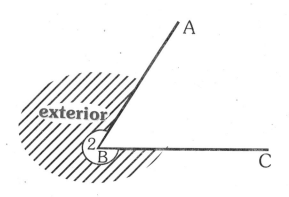

REVISION EXERCISE

1. Fill in the missing numbers :
   (a) 1,30,245, 1,30,345, _____, 1,30,545, _____, 1,30,745, _____ .
   (b) 1,26,080, 1,36,080, _____, 1,56,080, 1,66,080, _____, _____ .

2. (a) 2,56,374   (b) 5,70,658   (c)   251.06
      + 2,16,825   − 5,25,947   + 139.98
      _____   _____   _____

3. Write three equivalent fractions for each of these :
   (a) $\frac{1}{9}$ (b) $\frac{3}{4}$ (c) $\frac{2}{5}$ (d) $\frac{5}{6}$

4. (a) ____ x 5 = 140   (b) 100 x ____ = 700   (c) ____ x 7 = 630

5. (a) A metal rod 45 cm long is cut into 6 parts. What is the length of each part ?

   (b) A farmer had 192 chickens. Each day he sold 16 chickens. After how many days did he sell all the chickens ?

6. Change the following to tenths and then write as decimals.
   (a) $\frac{1}{5}$ (b) $\frac{2}{5}$ (c) $\frac{1}{2}$ (d) $\frac{3}{5}$

7. Write these numbers in order of size, putting the smallest first :
   0.45,   0.54,   4.05,   5.04

8. (a) Write 4 common multiples of 4 and 5.
   (b) Find the H.C.F. and L.C.M. of 18 and 24.

9. A shopkeeper paid Rs 2716 for 28 bicycles. How much did he pay for each bicycle ?

10. A bag of rice weighs $58\frac{3}{8}$ kg. A bag of sugar weighs $29\frac{1}{4}$ kg. What is their total weight ?

11. Divide a string 85.95 m long into 15 equal parts. What is the length of one piece ?

12. (a) 0.48 x 10   (b) 3.86 x 100   (c) 1 ÷ 10   (d) 1.2 ÷ 100

13. For each set write the fraction that shows the part which is coloured.
   (a)   (b)   (c)

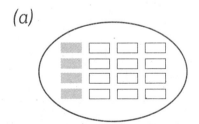
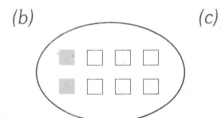
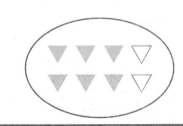

14. (a) 0.5 ÷ 10   (b) 0.5 ÷ 100   (c) 32.7 ÷ 3   (d) 96.3 ÷ 9

15. (a) 46.9 x 16   (b) 0.89 x 10   (c) 14.79 x 100   (d) 7.06 x 100

16. (a) 9.736 = _____ units ____ tenths ____ hundredths ____ thousandths

(b) $0.96 = \frac{9}{\square} + \frac{6}{\square}$ (c) $0.26 = \frac{2}{\square} + \frac{6}{\square}$

(d) What is the place value of 9 in 1.09 ?

17. Draw a line that is $\frac{2}{5}$ of AB.

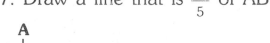

A ————————————————————————— B

18. $\frac{2}{3}$ of a class of 42 pupils wear spectacles.
How many pupils wear spectacles ?

19. Change to mixed numbers.

(a) $\frac{28}{5}$ (b) $\frac{97}{7}$ (c) $\frac{31}{8}$ ·(d) $\frac{76}{5}$

20. 7 boys divide 12 bars of chocolate equally among
themselves. How much   does each boy get ?

21. Complete the following.

(a) The highest common factor of 15 and 30 is _____.

(b) The lowest common multiple of 4 and 5 is _____.

(c) The product of 8 and 9 is _____.

22. The cost of one dress is Rs 266.75. What is the cost of 24 such dresses ?

23. (a) 746 x 43   (b) 636 x 91   (c) 793 ÷ 24   (d) 641 ÷ 14

24. Write three more fractions that belong to each set.

(a) $\frac{4}{5} = \frac{8}{10} =$ ____ = ____ = ____.

(b) $\frac{3}{7} = \frac{9}{21} =$ ____ = ____ = ____.

25. Find the difference between 36.72 and 26.98.

26. This picture shows a circle divided into
4 equal parts by two straight lines. What

27. Do these sums.

(a) 4 kg 750 g   (b) 4 kg   0 g   (c) 6 h 28 min   (d) 5 h 17 mm
   +2 kg 410 g   —2 kg 700 g   —3 h 36 min   —2 h 38 min
   _____   _____   _____   _____

   _____   _____   _____   _____

28. (a) Change $\frac{28}{3}$ and $\frac{56}{6}$ to mixed numbers.

(b) $2\frac{1}{3} + 1\frac{5}{6} =$ ___   (c) $3\frac{3}{8} - 1\frac{1}{4} =$ ___   (d) $4\frac{2}{3} -$ ___ $= 1\frac{5}{6}$

29. (a) During a football match, two-thirds of the 9000 tickets were sold. How many tickets were not sold ?

(b) There are 224 glasses in a box. How many glasses are there in 18 boxes?

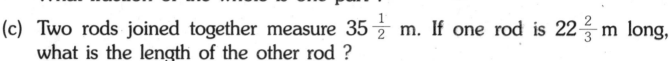

30. (a) Which is less, $\frac{3}{4}$ or $\frac{2}{3}$?

(b) A piece of stick is divided into 12 equal parts. What fraction of the whole is one part ?

(c) Two rods joined together measure $35\frac{1}{2}$ m. If one rod is $22\frac{2}{3}$ m long, what is the length of the other rod ?

31. Draw a line 12 cm long. Draw another line which is $\frac{3}{4}$ the length of the first line. What is the length of the second line ?

32. In the morning 3,254 people came to the post office. In the afternoon 578 people came.

(a) How many people came to the post office altogether ?

(b) How many more people came in the morning than in the afternoon ?

33. Arrange in order of size from the smallest to the largest.

0.46,   0.04,   0.4,   0.64,   4.6,   0.046

34. Change to decimal fractions.

(a) $17\frac{2}{5}$ (b) $38\frac{3}{4}$ (c) $45\frac{3}{5}$ (d) $78\frac{1}{2}$

35. Tom posted 14 parcels each weighing 0.98 kg.

What was the total weight of the parcels ?

36. A man spent Rs 65 buying fruits. He bought apples for $\frac{2}{5}$ of the money. How much did he pay for the apples ? How much did he pay for the rest of the fruits ?

37. (a) Colour 0.86 of this square   (b) Colour $\frac{2}{5}$ of this set.

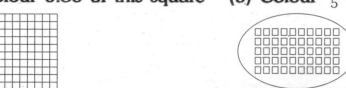
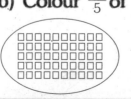

38. Rewrite the following sentence using numerals, instead of words, where possible.
There were eight thousand, three hundred and sixty-seven spectators at the football match.

39. Which is larger, 3,81,046 or 3,18,406 ?

40. Do these :
(a) 2,31,468 + 52031   (b) 1,24,673 — 1,13,463

41. Share 448 oranges equally among 28 people.

42. (a) $\frac{3}{8} + \frac{3}{16} =$ ___   (b) $1\frac{1}{2} + 1\frac{1}{8} =$ ___

43. (a) A piece of string is 154 cm long. It is formed from 6 pieces of string of the same length. What is the length of each piece ?
(b) Complete: 63, 56, ___, 42, ___, ___, 21, ___, 7.

44. Complete the following.
0.672 = _____ tenths, _____ hundredths and ____ thousandths.

45. What are the common factors of 32 and 36 ?

46. A number multiplied by itself is 64. What is the number ?

47. Write the following in fraction form.
(a) 0.4   (b) 2.1
(c) 10.2   (d) 26.3

48. Find the highest common factor of 16 and 24.

49. A factory employs 2 150 people. 484 travel by car, 1 450 by bus and the rest by motor scooter. How many people travel by motor scooter ?

50. Draw a line 9 cm long. Divide the line into parts each of which is $1\frac{1}{2}$ cm in length. How many parts are there ?

51. A string was cut into 24 equal pieces. Each piece was 2.25 m long. What was the length of the string before it was cut ?

52. Mrs. Gupta bought 6 tins of milk at Rs 102.95 a tin. How much did the 6 tins of milk cost altogether ?

53. Complete these.
(a) 9 thousands, 5 hundreds, 2 tens and 15 units is _____.
(b) 9 units, 4 tenths, 1 hundredth and 12 thousandths is _____.
(c) 80 hundreds, 4 tens, 9 units and 6 tenths is _____.

54. (a) $\frac{5}{9} = \frac{45}{\Box}$ (b) $\frac{4}{7} = \frac{32}{\Box}$ (c) $\frac{1}{3}$ of 33 = $\Box$ (d) $\frac{2}{5}$ of 25 = $\Box$

55. Complete these sentences.

(a) An improper fraction is a fraction whose numerator is ....

(b) A proper fraction is a fraction whose numerator is ....

(c) A mixed number is the sum of a ....

56. Complete this table.

Common fractions	$\frac{72}{100}$		$\frac{3}{4}$		$9\frac{2}{5}$			$\frac{7}{20}$
Decimal fractions	0.72	0.061		8.803		10.3	9.12	

57. (a) 0.6 + 0.8 = $\Box$ (b) 1.6 — 0.8 = $\Box$ (c) 3.5 — =1.6 $\Box$

(d) 0.9 + $\Box$ = 2.3 (e) 3.6 — 2.08 = $\Box$ (f) 2.9 + 5.62 = $\Box$

58. (a) 0.09 x 100 (b) 2.06 x 10 (c) 0.86 x 100 (d) 0.58 x 10

(e) 0.6 ÷ 10 (f) 0.8 ÷ 100 (g) 1.3 ÷ 10 (h) 4.78 ÷ 100

59. Write the first ten multiples of 8 and 16 and find their common multiples and the lowest common multiple.

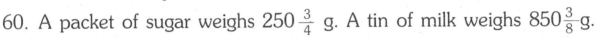

60. A packet of sugar weighs $250\frac{3}{4}$ g. A tin of milk weighs $850\frac{3}{8}$ g.

(a) What is the total weight of these two items ?

(b) Which is heavier, and by how much ?

61. (a) 236 ÷ 14 = ____ (b) 949 ÷ 7 = ____ (c) 72 ÷ 19= ____

(d) A boy paid Rs 7.25 for 29 postage stamps which were all alike. How much did he pay for each stamp ?

62. Write the number that is 1000 more than each of the following :

(a) 1,12,576 (b) 2,13,107 (c) 5,55,560 (d) 3,26,754

63. Write the numeral that means :

(a) 23 hundreds and 25 units (b) 153 hundreds and 8 tens.

64. Share 38 apples among 12 boys.

How much does each boy get ?

65. Change $7\frac{25}{28}$ into an improper fraction.

66. Krishna has 1,650 rubber bands. He shares it among 30 boys. How many rubber bands did each boy get ?

67. Write the following in numerals :
Twenty-three lakh, forty thousand, four hundred and six.

68. Which is smaller, 2,65,340 or 5,62,034 ?

69. Do these :

(a)   264935
    + 956244
_____

(b)   673286
    − 394512
_____

70. Find the value of:

(a) $6 \times \frac{1}{3}$ (b) $7 \times \frac{1}{2}$ (c) $9 \times \frac{1}{5}$ (d) $8 \times \frac{2}{3}$

(e) $15 \times \frac{1}{3}$ (f) $26 \times \frac{1}{2}$ (g) $39 \times \frac{1}{4}$ (h) $11 \times \frac{5}{8}$

71. 216 television parts are packed in boxes, each containing 18 parts. How many boxes are there ?

72. This chart shows the population of four towns.

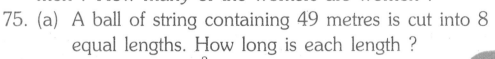

	town A	town B	town C	town D
Population	52354	61058	24232	91508

(a) Arrange these places in order of size, beginning with the smallest town.

(b) What is the total population of the four towns ?

73. A boy was $98\frac{3}{5}$ cm tall a few years ago. Now his height is $105\frac{11}{16}$ cm. How much taller has he grown ?

74. An electronic company employs 3057 workers. Two-thirds of the workers are men. How many of the workers are men ? How many of the workers are women ?

75. (a) A ball of string containing 49 metres is cut into 8 equal lengths. How long is each length ?

(b) A bag holds $12\frac{3}{4}$ kilograms of sugar. What is the weight of 9 bags of sugar ?

76. 23640 letters were sorted in a post office in one day. 38573 letters were sorted on the next day. How many letters were sorted in the two days ?

77. How much is 0.75 of Rs 50 ?

78. Multiply 378.9 by 36.

79. Mrs. Verma shared 5 oranges among 10 children. What fraction of an orange did each child get ?

80. This column graph shows the amount of money a boy spent each day of a week.

(a) On which day did he spend half the amount he spent on Monday ?

(b) On which day did he spend the most ?

(c) What was the total amount he spent during the six days ?

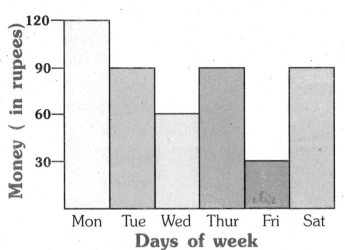

81.

(a) hours	minutes	(b) weeks	days	(c) years	months
23	38	8	2	25	7
— 19	54	— 5	5	— 18	11

82. (a) 8589 g — 3746 g= _____ (b) 6051m — 3593m= _____

83. (a) A tank is filled with water in $1\frac{5}{6}$ hours. It is emptied in $\frac{11}{12}$ hour.

What is the difference in the times taken to fill and empty the tank ?

(b) A tin contains 3 litres of cooking oil. A cook uses $8\frac{1}{2}$ tins each day. How many litres of oil are used each day ?

84. (a) Measure the length and width of this rectangle.

(b) Find the perimeter.

85. A motorist uses $8\frac{2}{3}$ litres of petrol each day. How much petrol does he use in a week ?

86. The weights of four babies are 4.3 kg, 11.2 kg, 7.5 kg and 3.8 kg. What is their average weight ?

87. Two oil drums can hold 580 litres of oil. How many litres can 9 oil drums of the same size hold ?

88. What is $\frac{1}{12}$ of 144 ?

89. How many days are there in 5 weeks ?

90. How many seconds are there in $7\frac{2}{3}$ minutes ?

Chapter-1. What We Have Learnt

A.
1. Nine hundred and ninety-nine
2. Nine thousand five hundred and ninety-three
3. Eight thousand five hundred and sixty-five
4. Four thousand and twenty-five
5. Fifty thousand six hundred and fifty-seven
6. Ninety-nine thousand nine hundred and ninety-nine

B.
1.	7070	2.	9009
3.	5907	4.	7542
5.	84911	6.	99999
7.	79840	8.	70909
9.	80089		

C.
1.	7070	2.	9999
3.	4753	4.	13842
5.	64802	6.	8988

D.
1.	10	2.	99
3.	100	4.	999
5.	1000	6.	9999
7.	10000	8.	99999

E.
a.
1. 4000+900+6
2. 9000+700+90
3. 70000+600+40+2

b.
4. 70924
5. 36800
6. 67342

F.
1. **in the ascending order**
709 < 907 < 3412 < 4321
in the descending order
4321 > 3412 > 907 > 709

2. **in the ascending order**
23085 < 27935 < 58053 < 58503
in the descending order
58503 > 58053 > 27935 > 23085

3. **in the ascending order**
26402 < 46204 < 54620 < 84206
in the descending order
84206 > 54620 > 46204 > 26402

G.
1. five-sixths
2. two-elevenths
3. three-thirteenths
4. One-eighth

H.
1.	7	8	7	6	6
2.	0	1	4	3	
3.	9	0	9	4	
4.	4	5	6		
5.	1	0			
6.	9	5			
7.	1	1	5		
8.	9	2	2		

I.
| a. | $\frac{5}{8}$ | b. | $\frac{2}{9}$ |
| c. | $\frac{4}{5}$ | d. | $\frac{29}{36}$ |

J.
a. 17800 b. 45990
c. 0

K.
b. 11:05 a.m.
c. 3:30 a.m.
d. 7:15 p.m.
e. 1:35 p.m.
f. 9:50 p.m.

L.
b. 4:00 p.m.
c. 7:45 a.m.
d. 5:00 p.m.
e. 5:00 a.m.
f. 11:50 a.m.

M.
b. 2:40 a.m.
c. 9:00 a.m.
d. 9:00 p.m.
e. 4:30 p.m.
f. 1:05 a.m.

N.
a. a.m.
b. p.m.
c. p.m.
d. a.m.

Chapter-2. Numeration And Notation (Indian system)

I.
a. 28,67,537
b. 57,75,819
c. 3,08,743
d. 25,01,749
e. 9,09,009

II.
f.	3100308	3874643
	3850784	5103731
g.	4037009	8673742
	4345471	9999999
h.	3507286	4251576
	4013821	7825482

III.
| I. | 4000003 | 3237503 |
| | 3426871 | 3000004 |

j.	4546445	4545545
	4545554	4545445
k.	6336363	3663363
	3663636	3636366

IV.	l.	6646632	6656632
	m.	8223611	9213711

V.

n. Three lakh ninety-nine thousand and forty-five

o. Five lakh seventy-five thousand nine hundred and eight

p. Five lakh eighty-three thousand and eighty-nine

q. Forty-eight lakh ninety-seven thousand two hundred and five

r. Ninety-nine lakh four thousand and fifty

s. Seventy-eight lakh ninety thousand eight hundred and ninety-two

t. Eighty-three lakh seven thousand nine hundred and eighty-five

u. Eighty-five lakh ninety-three thousand and seventy-three

v. Seventy-nine lakh twenty thousand one hundred and fourteen

w. Eighty-seven lakh ninety-two thousand and thirteen

x. Thirty lakh seventy-nine thousand six hundred and fifty-two

Chapter-3. Expanded Form And Place Value

7.	3	4	6	2	8	1
8.	5	2	4	3	6	0
9.	2	0	6	4	7	2
10.	5	6	0	3	2	9
11.	6	3	2	0	4	8

12.
a. two hundred
b. three hundred
c. four hundred and fifty
d. seven hundred and ten
e. four hundred and twenty-three
f. five hundred and three
g. two hundred and forty-seven
h. five hundred and sixty

13.
a. three thousand
b. four thousand
c. five thousand six hundred
d. five thousand two hundred and seventy
e. six thousand three hundred and twenty-four
f. five thousand three hundred and seven
g. six thousand eight hundred and ninety-three
h. two thousand seven hundred and fourteen

14.
a. 2,35,686
b. 5,60,494
c. 3,45,058
d. 6,73,205

15.
a. 7 thousand
b. 7 ten thousand
c. 7 lakh

16.
a. 6 ten
b. 6 hundred
c. 6 units

17.
a. 4 lakh
b. 4 ten thousand
c. 4 thousand

18.
a. 2 thousand
b. 2 lakh
c. 2 units

19.
a. 1 ten thousand
b. 1 ten
c. 1 unit

20.	400	21.	70
22.	3,00,000	23.	1,11,110
24.	1,11,101	25.	1,11,011
26.	1,01,111	27.	11,111

G.

28.
a. 1,00,000+20,000+4,000+600+70+3
b. 4,00,000+70,000+1,000+200+30+6
c. 7,00,000+10,000+4,000+600+30+2

29.
a. 2,00,000+20,000+2,000+20+2
b. 2,00,000+2,000+200+20+2
c. 2,00,000+20,000+200+20+2

30.
a. 2,00,000+20,000+2,000+200+2
b. 2,00,000+20,000+2,000+200+20+2
c. 2,00,000+20,000+2,000+200+20

31.
a. 3,00,000+800+70+1
b. 3,00,000+50,000+2,000+1
c. 3,00,000+50,000+70+1

32.
a. 4,00,000+90+1
b. 4,00,000+60,000+6,000+1
c. 4,00,000+60,000+2,000+6

33.	5,28,469	34.	63,71,258
35.	52,44,569	36.	81,02,535
37.	25,20,582		

38.	12	15	14	13	25
39.	15	17	11	10	17

J.
- a. 832049   b. 2452361
- c. 3217487   d. 316723
- e. 300524   f. 6508928

K.
- a. 213456   b. 2374298
- c. 405612   d. 6729468
- e. 342798   f. 1259406
- g. 2729486   h. 1813425
- i. 205946

L.
- a. 343529, 543529, 2443529, 5243529
- b. 382850, 392850, 2362850, 5372850
- c. 365825, 368825, 1367825, 3362825
- d. 453246, 453646, 2453746, 4453446
- e. 421207, 428207, 5428107, 8421107
- f. 234517, 234527, 1234627, 2234617
- g. 428566, 428586, 3428536, 9428576
- h. 361492, 361494, 2361493, 6361498
- i. 270952, 278052, 2208952, 9278902
- j. 364002, 364500, 1300572, 5304502

Chapter-4. Addition and Subtraction

A.

1. a. 27,74,985 b. 44,78,939 c. 5,59,658 d. 8,88,888
2. a. 67,94,997 b. 7,07,297 c. 7,58,866 d. 44,87,449
3. a. 75,47,779 b. 7,95,897 c. 6,85,937 d. 26,69,949
4. a. 72,82,899 b. 7,06,906 c. 6,45,382 d. 77,77,779

B.

1. a. 3,56,593 b. 15,78,617 c. 3,60,589 d. 5,43,694
2. a. 5,71,646 b. 11,78,777 c. 12,90,648 d. 17,75,563
3. a. 11,57,621 b. 6,67,182 c. 3,47,229 d. 6,87,945

C.

1. a. 37,79,881 b. 56,99,194 c. 66,92,861 d. 56,20,001
2. a. 72,65,862 b. 67,27,611 c. 89,83,291 d. 13,76,343
3. a. 56,69,321 b. 68,95,280 c. 87,80,551 d. 65,48,981

D.

1. a. 1,21,111 b. 16,33,353 c. 2,32,106 d. 11,22,136
2. a. 1,35,244 b. 25,23,220 c. 4,32,414 d. 23,12,461
3. a. 2,61,122 b. 52,31,310 c. 1,11,243 d. 20,42,852
4. a. 1,31,234 b. 28,32,221 c. 1,11,225 d. 32,23,111
5. a. 3,11,311 b. 22,53,413 c. 8,42,240 d. 12,12,571

E.

1. a. 2,84,128 b. 1,33,154 c. 3,79,722 d. 1,09,212
2. a. 2,38,568 b. 1,12,843 c. 92,082 d. 4,31,129
3. a. 1,32,174 b. 21,716 c. 5,09,671 d. 2,09,093

F.

1. a. 31,53,758 b. 11,26,268 c. 31,51,942 d. 71,57,112
2. a. 51,95,116 b. 41,29,212 c. 22,34,917 d. 21,11,085

3. a. 21,21,249
    b. 72,31,758
    c. 23,26,344
    d. 10,79,622

G.

a.

15	10	35
40	20	0
5	30	25

(60)

b.

4	19	16
25	13	1
10	7	22

(39)

c.

20	95	80
125	65	5
50	35	110

(195)

d.

66	6	90
78	54	30
18	102	42

(162)

H. **1.** **Complete the addition puzzles.**

a.

42	26	68
23	31	54
65	57	122

b.

204	115	319
322	233	555
526	348	874

2. **Complete the subtraction puzzles.**

a.

79	31	48
40	4	36
39	27	12

b.

357	120	237
110	100	10
247	20	227

3.

Sum			Difference
15	9+6	9-6	3
7	5+2	5-2	3
9	9+0	9-0	9
12	8+4	8-4	4
18	9+9	9-9	0
20	11+9	11-9	2
25	22+3	22-3	19
27	22+5	22-5	17

I.
1. a. 8,42,134   b. 55,65,647
    c. 37,82,644   d. 62,34,241
2. a. 10,02,326   b. 8,64,357
    c. 72,71,496   d. 83,17,334
3. a. 71,14,123   b. 8,63,838
    c. 62,14,488   d. 94,23,472

4. a. 10,02,341   b. 13,63,335
    c. 1,10,75,644   d. 1,34,36,543
5. a. 1,16,522   b. 8,11,735
    c. 11,35,670   d. 6,80,641
6. a. 1,76,947   b. 1,73,653
    c. 7,72,832   d. 37,70,810
7. a. 1,88,536   b. 13,68,871
    c. 2,97,269   d. 3,56,580
8. a. 1,66,227   b. 48,05,202
    c. 46,85,508   d. 46,187
9. a. 6,535   b. 54,34,018
    c. 83,655   d. 6,11,624
10. a. 41,59,036   b. 61,42,256
    c. 35,49,267   d. 46,87,547
11. a. 67,91,109   b. 66,79,099
    c. 44,25,893   d. 63,72,361
12. a. 54,40,131   b. 63,30,827
    c. 8,45,825   d. 9,65,554
13. a. 6,05,423   b. 8,25,668
    c. 6,07,635   d. 8,26,137
14. a. 10,21,131   b. 9,49,334
    c. 86,07,616   d. 6,72,211
15. a. 1,38,711   b. 17,43,123
    c. 57,729   d. 34,41,521
16. a. 45,86,521   b. 2,87,753
    c. 26,40,422   d. 52,548
17. a. 8,36,891   b. 2,65,775
    c. 5,58,861   d. 67,889
18. a. 8,78,675   b. 2,66,857
    c. 7,66,555   d. 1,75,686

Chapter 5. Multiplication & Division

I.
1.	1411261	2.	2216205
3.	2851479	4.	1993728
5.	2373120	6.	6822266
7.	1012320	8.	367605
9.	249840	10.	176710
11.	522000	12.	490793

II.
13.	1801968	14.	3413925
15.	3524220	16.	503334
17.	499506	18.	442197
19.	8855458	20.	3842265
21.	627984	22.	121770
23.	1434376	24.	2727621
25.	2862445	26.	456264
27.	4174015	28.	1152706
29.	1302825	30.	6305232
31.	4314282	32.	931728
33.	7375788	34.	3166838
35.	4672683	36.	4968852
37.	4915820 kg	38.	Rs 2677136
39.	Rs 7537530	40.	6617262 metres
41.	Rs 4074441	42.	1886586

| 43. | 4881245 biscuits |
| 44. | Rs 975374 |

45. a. 3 2 9 3
    b. 6 9

46. a. 680625
    b. 2618700
    c. 1205300

A.
1.	Q=23745	R=8
2.	Q=21782	R=7
3.	Q=8253	R=7
4.	Q=28993	R=65
5.	Q=17326	R=15
6.	Q=4058	R=20
7.	Q=7674	R=1
8.	Q=120031	R=41
9.	Q=40642	R=37

B.
10.	Q=5161	R=10
11.	Q=4407	R=21
12.	Q=4674	R=16
13.	Q=610	R=208
14.	Q=8053	R=5
15.	Q=4860	R=46
16.	Q=15498	R=44
17.	Q=1534	R=317
18.	Q=24429	R=16
19.	Q=6461	R=340
20.	Q=7413	R=229
21.	Q=39615	R=103
22.	Q=3706	R=319
23.	Q=10101	R=129
24.	Q=8364	R=445
25.	Q=2613	R=107
26.	Q=8766	R=2
27.	Q=2102	R=130
28.	Q=7833	R=535
29.	Q=18530	R=0
30.	Q=23148	R=63
31.	Q=1021	R=530
32.	Q=13022	R=342
33.	Q=9664	R=616

34. a. 3 3 1
    b. 2 8 1

35.	Rs 87328	
36.	Q=24038	R=191
37.	Rs 16685	
38.	25685 packets	

Chapter-6. Factors and Multiples

A. 1.
a.	2	3	b.	4	2
c	1	5	d.	2	6
e.	7	2	f.	3	5
g.	2	8	h.	6	4
i.	7	3			

2.
a.	2	b.	4
c.	1	d.	4
e.	8	f.	5
g.	2	h.	7
i.	3		

B. 1.
a.	1	7
b.	1	3
c.	2	4
d.	1	5
e.	1	9

3.

Product	Factors	Product	Factors
10	1,2,5,10	16	1,2, 4,8,16
11	1,11	18	1,2,3,6,9,18
14	1,2,7,14	20	1,2,4,5,10,20
15	1,3,5,15	24	1,2,3,4,6,8,12,24

4. a. two   b. two
   c. two   d. two
   e. two

Is a number always a factor of itself ?
Yes

5. **What is the number that is a factor of every number ?**
   1

C. 1.
a.	1	2	4
b.	4		
c.	5	10	20

2.
| a. | 1 | 2 |
| b. | 2 | |

3.
a.	CF =1,2	HCF =2
b.	CF =1,2	HCF =2
c.	CF =1,2,4	HCF =4
d.	CF =1,2,3,6	HCF =6
e.	CF =1,5	HCF =5
f.	CF =1,3	HCF =3
g.	CF =1,2	HCF =2
h.	CF =1,2,4,8	HCF =8
i.	CF =1,3	HCF =3
j.	CF =1,2,3,6	HCF =6
k.	CF =1,5	HCF =5
l.	CF =1,3,9	HCF =9
m.	CF =1,7	HCF =7
n.	CF =1,2,3,4,6,12	HCF =12
o.	CF =1,2,5,10	HCF =10
p.	CF =1,2,3,6	HCF =6
q.	CF =1,2,5,10	HCF =10
r.	CF =1,5	HCF =5

D.
1. 4, 8, 12, 16, 20, 24
2. 5, 10, 15, 20, 25, 30
3. 6, 12, 18, 24, 30, 36, 42
4. 4, 8, 12, 16, 20
5. 6, 12, 18, 24, 30
6. 6, 12, 18
7. 15, 30
8. 6, 12, 18

9.
a. 6   2
b. 9   2
c. 4   3
d. 6   3

E.
1.
a. 2,4,6,8,10,12,14,16,18,20
4,8,12,16,20,24,28,32,36,40
Common Multiples=4,8,12,16,20
L.C.M.= 4

b. 3,6,9,12,15,18,21,24,27,30
4,8,12,16,20,24,28,32,36,40
C.M.=12, 24
L.C.M.=12

c. 2,4,6,8,10,12,14,16,18,20
5,10,15,20,25,30,35,40,45,50
C.M.=10, 20
L.C.M.=10

d. 2,4,6,8,10,12,14,16,18,20
6,12,18,24,30,36,42,48,54,60
C.M.=6,12,18
L.C.M.=6

2.
a. 3,6,9,12,15,18,21,24,27,30
5,10,15,20,25,30,35,40,45,50
C.M.=15, 30
L.C.M.=15

b. 4,8,12,16,20,24,28,32,36,40
5,10,15,20,25,30,35,40,45,50
C.M.=20, 40
L.C.M.=20

c. same as 2 (a)
d. 4,8,12,16,20,24,28,32,36,40
6,12,18,24,30,36,42,48,54,60
C.M.=12,24,36
L.C.M.=12

3.
a. 4,8,12,16,20,24,28,32,36,40
8,16,24,32,40,48,56,64, 72,80
C.M.=8,16,24,32,40
L.C.M.=8

b. 3,6,9,12,15,18,21,24,27,30
9,18,27,36,45,54,63,72,81,90
C.M.=9,18,27
L.C.M.=9

c. 6,12,18,24,30,36,42,48,54,60

8,16,24,32,40,48,56,64,72,80
C.M.=24,48
L.C.M.=24

d. 5,10,15,20,25,30,35,40,45,50
10,20,30,40,50,60,70,80,90,100
C.M.=10,20,30,40,50
L.C.M.=10

4.
a. 3,6,9,12,15,18,21,24,27,30
12,24,36,48,60,72,84,96,108,120
C.M.=12, 24
L.C.M.=12

b. 4,8,12,16,20,24,28,32,36,40
12,24,36,48,60,72,84,96,108,120
C.M.=12,24,36
L.C.M.=12

c. 6,12,18,24,30,36,42,48,54,60
12,24,36,48,60,72,84,96,108,120
C.M.=12,24,36,48,60
L.C.M.=12

d. 8,16,24,32,40,48,56,64,72,80
12,24,36,48,60,72,84,96,108,120
C.M.=24,48,72
L.C.M.=24

5.
a. 8,10,12,14,18,24,30,32,36
b. 12,18,21,24,27,30,36
c. 8,12,24,32,36
d. 10,30
e. 12,18,24,30,36
f. 14,21
g. 8,24,32
h. 18,27,36

G.
1.
a. factor
b. product
c. multiple
2. 4   16
3. 16   32   44
4. 18   24   36
5. 6,9,12,15,18,21,27
12,18,24,30,36,42,54
a. 6,12,18,24
b. 6
6. 6
7.
a. 1,3   b.   1
c. 18   d.   3
e. 12
8. factors of 12 : 2,3,4,6
factors of 24 : 2,3,4,6,8,12
a. 1,2,3,4,6,12
b. 12
9. 1,5,7,35

Chapter-7.
More About Fractions

A. **1.** a. $1\frac{1}{6}$ b. $1\frac{3}{8}$
c. $1\frac{3}{4}$ d. $1\frac{4}{5}$
e. $1\frac{7}{8}$ f. $1\frac{5}{12}$

2. a. $\frac{3}{2}$ b. $\frac{7}{4}$
c. $\frac{6}{5}$ d. $\frac{5}{2}$
e. $\frac{17}{8}$ f. $\frac{26}{12}$

B.
	a.	b.	c.
1.	$\frac{1}{2}$	$\frac{7}{8}$	$\frac{11}{12}$
2.	$\frac{13}{15}$	$\frac{2}{3}$	$\frac{4}{5}$
3.	1	1	$\frac{2}{5}$
4.	0	0	$\frac{1}{3}$
5.	$\frac{1}{4}$	$\frac{1}{4}$	$\frac{1}{8}$
6.	$\frac{1}{3}$	$\frac{1}{3}$	$\frac{11}{15}$
7.	$\frac{2}{21}$	$\frac{2}{21}$	$\frac{107}{168}$
8.	$\frac{1}{3}$	$\frac{1}{3}$	$\frac{2}{3}$

C.
1. a. $2,\ \frac{5}{8}$ b. $3,\ \frac{5}{9}$
2. a. $2,\ \frac{1}{10}$ b. $3,\ \frac{2}{9}$
3. a. $2,\ \frac{1}{4}$ b. $4,\ \frac{7}{10}$

D.
	a.	b.	c.
1.	$\frac{7}{10}$	$\frac{7}{12}$	$\frac{8}{15}$
2.	$\frac{11}{12}$	$\frac{9}{10}$	$\frac{5}{6}$
3.	$\frac{11}{15}$	$\frac{9}{20}$	$\frac{19}{20}$
4.	$\frac{3}{5}$	$\frac{13}{20}$	$\frac{14}{15}$
5.	$\frac{3}{10}$	$\frac{3}{10}$	$\frac{5}{12}$
6.	$\frac{1}{6}$	$\frac{1}{20}$	$\frac{13}{24}$
7.	$\frac{5}{12}$	$\frac{3}{30}$	$\frac{1}{4}$
8.	$\frac{1}{10}$	$\frac{7}{20}$	$\frac{1}{10}$
9.	$\frac{3}{20}$	$\frac{3}{10}$	$\frac{1}{20}$

E.
	a	b	c
1.	$7\frac{1}{4}$	$2\frac{1}{2}$	$3\frac{2}{3}$
2.	$2\frac{3}{4}$	$2\frac{3}{8}$	$2\frac{1}{2}$
3.	$36\frac{3}{4}$	$55\frac{4}{5}$	$49\frac{5}{8}$

	a.	b.	c.
1.	$3\frac{1}{8}$	$4\frac{1}{6}$	$5\frac{1}{3}$
2.	$6\frac{1}{2}$	4	$4\frac{3}{8}$
3.	$4\frac{1}{8}$	6	$5\frac{5}{8}$
4.	$32\frac{3}{4}$	$81\frac{1}{8}$	$101\frac{7}{8}$

F.
1. a. $2\frac{1}{2}$ b. $1\frac{1}{4}$ c. $1\frac{2}{3}$
2. a. $1\frac{1}{4}$ b. $1\frac{1}{4}$ c. $2\frac{3}{8}$
3. $11\frac{1}{4}$ $10\frac{5}{8}$ $12\frac{1}{2}$ $11\frac{1}{2}$
4. $17\frac{3}{4}$ $34\frac{1}{6}$ $26\frac{3}{8}$ $38\frac{3}{8}$

	a.	b.	c.
1.	$1\frac{1}{2}$	$2\frac{3}{4}$	$1\frac{1}{3}$
2.	$1\frac{2}{3}$	$1\frac{3}{4}$	$1\frac{1}{2}$
3.	2	$2\frac{7}{8}$	$2\frac{5}{6}$
4.	$2\frac{2}{3}$	$2\frac{7}{8}$	$1\frac{7}{8}$

G.
1. 1 hr **2.** $2\frac{3}{4}$ hr
3. $2\frac{1}{2}$ m **4.** $2\frac{5}{8}$ m
5. $3\frac{1}{5}$ m **6.** $3\frac{1}{4}$ kg
7. $8\frac{1}{6}$ kg **8.** $7\frac{5}{8}$ min
9. $10\frac{1}{4}$ cups **10.** $7\frac{1}{4}$ litres
11. 80 sq, $27\frac{1}{2}$ sq, $52\frac{1}{2}$ sq
12. $1\frac{5}{6}$ m **13.** $\frac{5}{8}$
14. $6\frac{3}{8}$ m **15.** $\frac{2}{3}$

H.
1. a. $\frac{1}{2}$ b. $\frac{4}{5}$ c. $\frac{3}{4}$ d. $\frac{5}{8}$
2. a. $\frac{5}{6}$ b. $\frac{1}{3}$ c. $\frac{4}{9}$ d. $\frac{3}{5}$
3. a. $\frac{5}{2}$ b. $\frac{3}{2}$ c. $\frac{6}{5}$ d. $\frac{4}{3}$ e. 2 f. $\frac{8}{5}$

g. 2   h. $\frac{12}{5}$ i. $\frac{9}{8}$

j. $\frac{5}{4}$ k. 1   l. 2

4. $3\frac{1}{2}$ apples

5. $2\frac{1}{2}$ cups of milk

6. $\frac{5}{8}$ m   7. $1\frac{1}{4}$ hr

I. a. $\frac{1}{3}$ cm, $\frac{2}{3}$ cm

b. 5, 5 cm

c. 10 cm, 10 cm

1. a. 3   b. 4
   c. 2   d. 3
   e. 1   f. 5
   g. 3   h. 6
   i. 1   j. 2

2. a. 2   4
   b. 3   9
   c. 2   4   6   8
   d. 2   6   10   14

3. a. 6   b. 5   c. 4
4. a. 3   b. 3   c. 2
5. a. 8   b. 15   c. 6
6. a. 12   b. 12   c. 28
7. a. 12   b. 16   c. 21
8. a. 12   b. 16   c. 27
9. a. 9   b. 35   c. 27
10. a. 32   b. 24   c. 40
11. a. 24   b. 40   c. 45
12. a. 20   b. 80   c. 6

J.
1. a. Rs 18   b. 10 hr
2. a. Rs 27   b. 9 cm
3. a. 21 gm   b. 24 l
4. a. 32 min   b. 21 m
5. a. 40 sec   b. Rs 14
6. a. Rs 24   b. 45 l
7. a. 27 cm   b. Rs 48
8. a. 9 gm   b. 35 l
9. a. 30 sec   b. 28 hr
10. a. 45 min   b. 15 gm
11. 35 books
12. Rs 14
13. 9 m
14. 6 l
15. 27 books
16. 49 fishes

K.   1.
a.   proper fraction
b.   mixed number
c.   whole number

d.   improper fraction
e.   an object
f.   a set of objects
g.   numerator
h.   denominator

2. a. $\frac{3}{5}$ b. $\frac{1}{3}$
   c. $\frac{6}{8}$ d. $\frac{8}{12}$

3. a. $\frac{2}{8}$, $\frac{3}{12}$, $\frac{4}{16}$

   b. $\frac{2}{6}$, $\frac{3}{9}$, $\frac{4}{12}$

   c. $\frac{4}{10}$, $\frac{8}{20}$, $\frac{16}{40}$

   d. $\frac{6}{8}$, $\frac{9}{12}$, $\frac{12}{16}$

   e. $\frac{2}{10}$, $\frac{3}{15}$, $\frac{4}{20}$

4. a. 1   b. 1   c. 2
   d. 3   e. 4

5. a. $\frac{6}{12}$ or $\frac{1}{2}$

   b. $\frac{6}{21}$ or $\frac{2}{7}$

   c. $\frac{10}{16}$ or $\frac{5}{8}$

6. a. 7   b. 14   c. 21
   d. 20   e. 12   f. 18

7. a. $\frac{5}{2}$ or $2\frac{1}{2}$ b. $\frac{33}{8}$ or $4\frac{1}{8}$
   c. $\frac{9}{5}$ or $1\frac{4}{5}$ d. $\frac{101}{8}$ or $12\frac{5}{8}$
   e. $\frac{31}{2}$ or $14\frac{3}{2}$ f. 12

8. 100 cm

9   a.   unlike

$\frac{7}{8}$	$\frac{1}{2}$

$\frac{1}{4}$	$\frac{1}{5}$

$\frac{3}{4}$	$\frac{2}{5}$

$\frac{4}{7}$	$\frac{5}{8}$

$\frac{6}{11}$	$\frac{7}{13}$

b.   improper
$\frac{4}{3}$ $\frac{5}{4}$ $\frac{6}{5}$ $\frac{7}{6}$ $\frac{8}{7}$

c.   mixed
$1\frac{1}{2}$ $2\frac{1}{4}$ $3\frac{3}{4}$ $5\frac{1}{2}$ $6\frac{3}{4}$

d.   proper
$\frac{1}{4}$ $\frac{2}{3}$ $\frac{3}{4}$ $\frac{3}{5}$ $\frac{4}{7}$

10. $22\frac{5}{8}$ kg   **11.** 3 cm,1 cm

12. 10 marbles

13. $\frac{4}{5}$ m   **14.** $\frac{4}{5}$ chocolate

15. $2\frac{3}{8}$ m

16.
a. $<$ b. $<$
c. $<$ d. $=$
e. $=$ f. $>$

17. 3 m

18.
a. 10
b. 8
c. 4
d. 12

19. 4.5 cm

20. $1\frac{1}{3}$ apples

21.
a. $\frac{4}{16}$ or $\frac{1}{4}$ b. $\frac{3}{15}$ or $\frac{1}{5}$
c. $\frac{11}{16}$ d. $\frac{6}{8}$ or $\frac{3}{4}$

Exercise I

A.
1. $\frac{3}{20}$ **2.** $\frac{1}{8}$ **3.** $\frac{2}{9}$ **4.** $\frac{2}{17}$
5. $\frac{1}{22}$ **6.** $\frac{2}{55}$ **7.** $\frac{2}{49}$ **8.** $\frac{1}{7}$
9. $\frac{2}{55}$ **10.** $\frac{7}{65}$ **11.** $\frac{3}{49}$ **12.** $\frac{3}{58}$

B.
13. $\frac{1}{3}$ **14.** $\frac{3}{8}$ **15.** $\frac{2}{5}$
16. $\frac{3}{5}$ **17.** $\frac{7}{8}$ **18.** $\frac{2}{7}$
19. $\frac{2}{3}$ **20.** $\frac{13}{9}$ **21.** $\frac{5}{9}$
22. $\frac{4}{3}$ **23.** $\frac{5}{8}$ **24.** $\frac{1}{3}$
25. $\frac{3}{47}$ **26.** $\frac{3}{8}$ **27.** $\frac{1}{3}$
28. $\frac{3}{16}$ **29.** $\frac{25}{8}$ **30.** $\frac{155}{9}$

C.
31. $\frac{25}{28}$ **32.** $\frac{3}{2}$ **33.** $\frac{3}{5}$
34. $\frac{3}{2}$ **35.** $\frac{3}{2}$ **36.** $\frac{2}{3}$
37. $\frac{117}{125}$ **38.** $\frac{3}{4}$ **39.** $\frac{5}{3}$

D.
40. $\frac{7}{10}$ **41.** $\frac{8}{3}$ **42.** $\frac{33}{7}$
43. $\frac{36}{143}$ **44.** 26   **45.** $\frac{36}{5}$
46. $\frac{7}{6}$ **47.** $\frac{2}{5}$ **48.** $\frac{13}{3}$

49. $\frac{11}{2}$ **50.** $\frac{8}{3}$ **51.** 51

E. **52.** $\frac{10}{9}$ **53.** $\frac{5}{3}$ **54.** $\frac{910}{153}$
55. $\frac{35}{9}$ **56.** $\frac{7}{9}$ **57.** 12
58. $\frac{8}{13}$ **59.** $\frac{5}{14}$ **60.** $\frac{3}{4}$
61. $\frac{4225}{256}$ **62.** $\frac{3}{2}$ **63.** 6
64. 3   **65.** $\frac{51}{8}$ **66.** $\frac{35}{12}$
67. $\frac{3}{2}$

Exercise II

A.
1. $\frac{1}{2}$ **2.** $\frac{11}{27}$ **3.** $\frac{1}{5}$
4. $\frac{3}{5}$ **5.** $\frac{20}{27}$ **6.** $\frac{1}{3}$
7 $\frac{20}{3}$ **8.** $\frac{80}{9}$ **9.** 1
10. 21   **11.** 160   **12.** $\frac{25}{2}$

B.
13. $\frac{5}{3}$ **14.** $\frac{2}{9}$ **15.** 2
16. $\frac{25}{1092}$ **17.** $5\frac{5}{8}$ **18.** $\frac{361}{17}$
19. 109 vests   **20.** $\frac{8}{15} \div 5$

Chapter-8. Introduction to Decimal Fractions

A.1.
a. $\frac{4}{10} = 0.4$ b. $\frac{6}{10} = 0.6$
c. $2\frac{2}{10} = 2.2$ d. $3\frac{5}{10} = 3.5$
e. $5\frac{0}{10} = 5$ f. $7\frac{8}{10} = 7.8$

2.
a. $10\frac{4}{10} = 10.4$ b. $15\frac{2}{10} = 15.2$
c. $19\frac{3}{10} = 19.3$ d. $23\frac{5}{10} = 23.5$
e. $31\frac{1}{10} = 31.1$ f. $44\frac{8}{10} = 44.8$

3.
a. $\frac{8}{10} = 0.8$ b. $47\frac{3}{10} = 47.3$
c. $8\frac{9}{10} = 8.9$ d. $60\frac{5}{10} = 60.5$

4.

	Tens	Units	Tenths
a.	1	0	3
b.	1	6	7
c.	2	3	0
d.	3	4	5
e.	4	3	0

5.
a. $\frac{12}{16}$ or .75   b. $\frac{20}{20}$ or 1.0
c. $\frac{50}{50}$ or 1.0   b. $\frac{32}{32}$ or 1.0

g.	8	4	$\frac{84}{100}$
h.	9	6	$\frac{96}{100}$

6.
a.	2.3	b.	0.7	c.	5.6
d.	0.9	e.	8.2	f.	4.4
g.	7.2	h.	9.1	i.	10.3
j.	14.8	k.	18.1	l.	23.5

7.
a. $\frac{5}{10}$ b. $\frac{9}{10}$ c. $\frac{1}{10}$

d. $\frac{3}{10}$ e. $2\frac{6}{10}$ f. $3\frac{4}{10}$

g. $7\frac{2}{10}$ h. $6\frac{7}{10}$ i. $8\frac{4}{10}$

j. $10\frac{3}{10}$ k. $11\frac{7}{10}$ l. $13\frac{9}{10}$

8.
a. 3.6 cm or $3\frac{6}{10}$ cm

b. 5.2 cm or $5\frac{2}{10}$ cm

9.
a. 0.9 cm   b. $1\frac{8}{10}$ cm

c. $6\frac{5}{10}$ cm   d. 8.5 cm

e. $12\frac{3}{10}$ cm   f. $13\frac{5}{10}$ cm

g. $3\frac{3}{10}$ cm   h. $6\frac{7}{10}$ cm

i. $5\frac{0}{10}$ cm   j. $5\frac{8}{10}$ cm

k. $4\frac{3}{10}$ cm   l. $1\frac{2}{10}$ cm

B.
1.
a. $\frac{6}{100}$ or six hundredths

b. $\frac{17}{100}$ or seventeen hundredths

c. $\frac{30}{100}$ or thirty hundredths

d. $\frac{40}{100}$ or forty hundredths

e. $\frac{31}{100}$ or thirty-one hundredths

f. $\frac{68}{100}$ or sixty-eight hundredths

g. $\frac{86}{100}$ or eighty-six hundredths

h. $\frac{79}{100}$ or seventy-nine hundredths

3.
b.	0	8	$\frac{8}{100}$
c.	3	1	$\frac{31}{100}$
d.	5	0	$\frac{50}{100}$
e.	6	5	$\frac{65}{100}$
f.	7	2	$\frac{72}{100}$

4.
a.	0.15	b.	0.09
c.	0.08	d.	0.27
e.	1.30	f.	1.31
g.	1.62	h.	1.29
i.	2.53	j.	2.60
k.	3.75	l.	3.88
m.	2.08	n.	3.80
o.	2.51	p.	3.45

5.
a.	<	b.	=	c.	<
d.	>	e.	>	f.	=
g.	<	h.	>	i.	<

6.
a. 6 hundredths
b. 3 units
c. 3 tenths
d. 7 tens

C.
1.
a. 5 tenths
b. 5 hundreds
c. 5 hundredths
d. 5 thousands
e. 5 units
f. 5 thousandths

2.
b.	tenth	$\frac{7}{10}$
c.	tens	30
d.	hundreds	500
e.	thousandths	$\frac{9}{1000}$
f.	thousands	7000

3.
a.	0.254	b.	0.563
c.	0.843	d.	0.411
e.	0.309	f.	0.608
g.	0.273	h.	0.607
i.	0.532	j.	0.861
k.	0.188	l.	0.770

D.
1.
a.	0.03	b.	0.6
c.	0.009	d.	0.08

2.
a.	0.007	b.	0.15
c.	0.036	d.	1.8

3.
a.	0.27	b.	3.5
c.	0.015	d.	2.7

4.
a.	0.45	b.	0.098
c.	0.7	d.	0.07

5.
a.	3.8	b.	1.12
c.	3.42	d.	1.25

6.
a.	3.45	b.	11.2
c.	2.123	d.	1.367

7.
a.	15.75	b.	12.3
c.	4.218	d.	52.51

8.
a.	15.8	b.	12.86
c.	15.742	d.	9.219

9.   a. $2\frac{72}{100}$ b. $27\frac{2}{10}$

     c. $10\frac{7}{10}$ d. $1\frac{7}{100}$

10.   a. $3\frac{56}{100}$ b. $35\frac{6}{10}$

     c. $45\frac{63}{100}$ d. $45\frac{63}{100}$

11.   a. $17\frac{92}{100}$ b. $1\frac{792}{1000}$

     c. $5\frac{525}{1000}$ d. $55\frac{25}{100}$

12.   a. $157\frac{8}{10}$ b. $15\frac{78}{100}$

     c. $15\frac{78}{100}$ d. $18\frac{6}{100}$

13.   a. $18\frac{6}{100}$ b. $1\frac{806}{1000}$

     c. $25\frac{56}{100}$ d. $255\frac{6}{10}$

14.   a. $25\frac{56}{100}$ b. $27\frac{45}{100}$

     c. $2\frac{743}{1000}$ d. $274\frac{3}{10}$

15.   a. $5\frac{31}{100}$ b. $27\frac{68}{100}$

     c. $2\frac{476}{1000}$ d. $600\frac{5}{100}$

16.   a. $7\frac{413}{1000}$ b. $250\frac{7}{10}$

     c. $1\frac{125}{1000}$ d. $7\frac{425}{1000}$

17.   a. $\frac{5}{10}, \frac{6}{10}, \frac{8}{10}, \frac{9}{10}, \frac{10}{10}$

     b.   1.1, 1.2, 1.3, 1.4

     c. $\frac{10}{100}, \frac{11}{100}, \frac{12}{100}, \frac{13}{100}$

     d.   0.30, 0.31, 0.32, 0.34, 0.35
     e.   0.06, 0.07, 0.09, 0.10, 0.11
     f.   6 tenths, 8 tenths, 10 tenths
     g.   8 hundredths, 14 hundredths
     h.   0.54, 0.56, 0.58, 0.60
     i.   0.132, 0.135, 0.138, 0.141

     j. $\frac{60}{100}, \frac{65}{100}, \frac{70}{100}, \frac{75}{100}$

     k. $\frac{28}{1000}, \frac{30}{1000}$

     l.   3.6, 4.2, 4.5, 4.8, 5.1
     m.   1.90, 2.00, 2.05, 2.10, 2.15
     n.   3.686, 3.706, 3.716, 3.726, 3.736

18.   a.   0.3, 0.35, 0.53
     b.   0.4, 0.48, 0.84
     c.   0.2, 0.25, 0.52
     d.   0.69, 0.9, 0.96
     e.   0.7, 0.9, 0.97

     f.   0.89, 0.9, 0.98
     g.   1.2, 1.26, 1.62
     h.   3.45, 3.5, 3.54

19.   a.   0.3, 0.03, 0.003
     b.   0.8, 0.08, 0.008
     c.   1.6, 0.16, 0.016
     d.   2.21, 0.21, 0.021
     e.   42.5, 4.25, 0.425
     f.   63.1, 6.31, 0.631
     g.   0.321, 0.231, 0.123
     h.   0.986, 0.698, 0.689

E.   1.
     a.   0.25   b.   0.48
     c.   0.14   d.   0.37
     e.   0.91   f.   0.63
     g.   0.246   h.   0.537
     i.   0.196   j.   0.687
     k.   0.666   l.   0.731

2.   a. $\frac{1}{10} + \frac{5}{100}$ b. $\frac{3}{10} + \frac{7}{10}$

     c. $\frac{6}{10} + \frac{8}{100}$ d. $\frac{9}{10} + \frac{1}{100}$

     e. $\frac{2}{10} + \frac{1}{100} + \frac{5}{1000}$

     f. $\frac{3}{10} + \frac{6}{100} + \frac{9}{1000}$

     g. $\frac{4}{10} + \frac{8}{100} + \frac{5}{1000}$

     h. $\frac{3}{10} + \frac{7}{1000}$

     i. $\frac{5}{10} + \frac{6}{100} + \frac{7}{1000}$

     j. $\frac{7}{10} + \frac{9}{100} + \frac{8}{1000}$

     k. $\frac{9}{10} + \frac{2}{100} + \frac{2}{1000}$

     l. $\frac{8}{10} + \frac{6}{100} + \frac{4}{1000}$

3.   a.   1.35   b.   1.71
     c.   1.82   d.   2.59
     e.   2.63   f.   3.86
     g.   1.245   h.   1.963
     i.   2.957   j.   3.749

F.   1.
     a.   0.4 or 4 tenths
     b.   0.6 or 6 tenths
     c.   0.5 or 5 tenths
     d.   0.2 or 2 tenths
     e.   0.6 or 6 tenths
     f.   0.05 or 5 hundredths

g. 0.35 or 3 tenths + 5 hundredths
h. 0.85 or 8 tenths + 5 hundredths

2.
a.	1.5	b.	2.25
c.	3.2	d.	1.75
e.	2.4	f.	4.6
g.	1.35	h.	3.2
i.	3.45	j.	3.65
k.	8.6	l.	7.75
m.	4.75	n.	2.55
o.	4.55	p.	9.8

G.

1.
a.	$2\frac{4}{5}$	b.	$\frac{9}{10}$
c.	$3\frac{3}{10}$	d.	$\frac{7}{10}$

2.
a.	$\frac{4}{5}$	b.	$1\frac{1}{10}$
c.	$5\frac{2}{5}$	d.	$6\frac{1}{2}$

3.
a.	$\frac{1}{4}$	b.	$3\frac{3}{4}$
c.	$2\frac{4}{5}$	d.	$7\frac{7}{20}$

4.
a.	$\frac{13}{20}$	b.	$4\frac{1}{20}$
c.	$7\frac{1}{2}$	d.	$8\frac{9}{20}$

H. 3.

Common fractions	Decimals	Common fractions	Decimals
$\frac{1}{10}$	0.1	$\frac{1}{1000}$	0.001
$\frac{4}{1000}$	0.004	$\frac{7}{20}$	0.35
$\frac{3}{10}$	0.3	$\frac{1}{4}$	0.25
$\frac{10}{10}$	1.0	$\frac{100}{100}$	1.0

I.   1.
a.	0.6	b.	0.7
c.	0.9	d.	0.6
e.	0.8	f.	0.9
g.	0.7	h.	0.9
i.	0.8		

2.
a. 1.4 + 1.4 = 2.8
b. 1.5 + 1.4 = 2.9
c. 2.2 + 2.6 = 4.8
d. 2.6 + 1.1 = 3.7

3.
a. 0.3+0.9=1.2 or 0.9+0.3=1.2
b. 0.6+0.8=1.4 or 0.8+0.6=1.4
c. 0.4+0.9=1.3 or 0.9+0.4=1.3
d. 0.8+1.4=2.2 or 1.4+0.8=2.2
e. 1.5+0.9=2.4 or 0.9+1.5=2.4
f. 2.4+0.8=3.2 or 0.8+2.4=3.2

4.
a.	1.3	b.	2.4
c.	2.4	d.	2.3
e.	2.1	f.	2.2
g.	4.3	h.	3.7
i.	2.3	j.	14.8
k.	5.9	l.	4.5

J.   1.
a. 0.2+0.5=0.7 or 0.7-0.5=0.2
b. 0.4+0.7=1.1 or 1.1-0.7=0.4
c. 0.5+0.8=1.3 or 1.3-0.8=0.5
d. 0.7+0.8=1.5 or 1.5-0.7=0.8
e. 1.2+0.9=2.1 or 2.1-0.9=1.2
f. 1.6+1.6=3.2 or 3.2-1.6=1.6

2.
a.	1.5	b.	2.2
c.	2.2	d.	0.6
e.	1.8	f.	1.7
g.	3.6	h.	1.5
i.	2.7	j.	1.4
k.	1.7	l.	2.8

K.

1.
a.	29.33	b.	35.22
c.	51.41	d.	58.71

2.
a.	7.19	b.	5.26
c.	14.82	d.	28.65

3.
a.	40.13	b.	56.82
c.	63.65	d.	74.45

4.
a.	72.00	b.	81.96
c.	70.19	d.	85.30

L.

1.
a.	12.58	b.	15.77
c.	15.38	d.	16.56

2.
a.	26.29	b.	18.63
c.	28.22	d.	24.75

3.
a.	22.76	b.	24.72
c.	14.68	d.	42.29

4.
a.	7.27	b.	6.08
c.	12.75	d.	8.93

M.

1. 23.82
2. 32.66
3. 21.83

1.
a.	10.3	b.	46.6
c.	65.5	d.	46.36
e.	48.29	f.	70.07
g.	32.17	h.	36.58
i.	52.85	j.	2214.59
k.	57.58	l.	70.96

2.	a.	9.75	b.	10.37
	c.	3.79	d.	8.47
	e.	16.77	f.	22.57
	g.	8.48	h.	13.66
	i.	14.94	j.	5.45
	k.	31.47	l.	17.87

3.	a.	10.41	b.	8.95
	c.	8.52	d.	7.58
	e.	2.74	f.	1.92
	g.	8.12	h.	1.76
	i.	17.57	j.	14.29
	k.	6.14	l.	11.26

N.
1. 15 cm
2. 12.75 m
3. a. Perimeter =14.4 cm
   b. Difference in the length and the breadth=1.4 cm
4. Length of pencil A= 9.3 cm
   Length of pencil B= 6.7 cm
   a. 16 cm
   b. 2.6cm

5. Rs 6.90
6. Rs 22.05
7. 7.75 kg
8. Rs 3.35
9. 1.55 m
10. 7.9 m
11. 20.31 m
12. 1.2 m
13. 2.95 kg
14. a. 2.11 kg
    b. 0.15 kg
15. 8.54 m
16. 3.25 kg
17. 40.2 kg

Chapter-9. Graphs
1.	a.	May
	b.	January and March
	c.	18 cars
	d.	April and June
	e.	120 cars

2.	a.	C
	b.	D
	c.	A and E
	d.	60 min
	e.	1 hr 40 min
	f.	C
	g.	2 hr
	h.	7 hr 20 min

5.	a.	25 lit
	b.	Wed and Sat
	c.	Fri and Sun
	d.	Wed and Sat
	e.	20 lit
	f.	20 lit
	g.	Tue, Fri and Sun

Chapter-10. Circles
B.
3. 4 cm, 7 cm

C.
1.	a.	440 cm
	b.	220 cm
	c.	176 cm
	d.	88 cm

2.	a.	131.88 cm
	b.	28.26 cm
	c.	62.172 cm
	d.	35.168 cm

3. Read second 'circumference' as diameter.
	a.	19.7192 cm
	b.	49.298 cm
	c.	78.8768 cm
	d.	177.4728 cm

4. 94.2 cm
5. 110 m
6. 528 cm
7. 235.84 cm, 235.84 m
9. d. Any number
10.	a.	Longest
	b.	Same
	c.	Diameter
	d.	Two
	e.	Chord

D.
1.	a	78.50 cm^2
	b.	200.96 cm^2
	c.	113.04 m^2
	d.	19.6250 m^2
	e.	1.1304 m^2
	f.	4.5196 m^2

2.	a.	616 cm^2
	b.	38.50 cm^2
	c.	346.5 cm^2

3.	a.	28 cm
	b.	8 cm
	c.	1.4 m
	d.	7 m

4. 346.5 cm²
5. 1386 m²
6. 38.5 cm²   7. $160\frac{2}{7}$ cm²
8. 77 cm²
9. 44 cm
10. 154 cm²
11. 346.5 cm²
12. 616 m²
13. a. Arc
    b. Diameter
    c. Radius
    d. Sector
    e. Circular
    f. Circumference
    g. Segment

Chapter 11. Angles

A. 1. a. ∠LNO, ∠LNM, ∠ONM
      b. Read 'O' in the centre
         ∠POS, ∠POR, ∠ROQ, ∠SOQ
      c. ∠BGH, ∠BGF, ∠OBG, ∠ABG, ∠OBC, ∠BOE, ∠FGH, ∠ABC
      d. ∠ABC, ∠BAC, ∠ACB

2. a. a°
   b. b°
   c. ∠BCD
   d. ∠CDF

C.
1 a. ∠ABC=45°
   b. ∠PQR=70°
   c. ∠XYZ=125°
   d. ∠MNP=115°
   e. ∠X=32°
   f. ∠a=90°
      ∠b=90°
      ∠c=90°
      ∠d=90°

2. a. ∠a+∠b=120°+60°=180°
   b. ∠A+∠B+∠C=60°+60°+60°=180°
   c. ∠a+∠b+∠c+∠d=140°+145°+40°+35° =360°

E.
1. a. Acute angle
   b. Right angle
   c. Obtuse angle
   d. Reflex angle
   e. Straight angle
2. a. Acute angle
   b. Reflex angle
   c. Obtuse angle
   d. Acute angle
   e. Right angle ·

F.
1. a. Adjacent angles
   b. Adjacent angles
   c. Angles at a point
   d. Vertically opposite angles
   e. Straight angle
   f. Reflex angle

2. a. x°=20   b. y°=60

Chapter-12. Triangles

E.
1. a. a°=78   b. b°=76
   c. c°=60   d. d°=38
   e. e°=35   f. f°=45
   g. g°=25

2. a. a,b,c   b. e,g
   c. d,f   d. a,d,e
   e. c   f. b,f,g

3. a. three   b. three
   c. equal   d. two
   e. two   f. two

4. a. △AEC, △ABC, △AFE
   b. △ACE
   c. △ABC, △AFE
   d. △ABC, △CDE
   e. △ABC

5. 45° each   6. 60° each

7. 30°each   8. 55°

12.

∠A=55°BC=3.5cm	∠D=35° EF=2.5cm	∠G=115° HI=5cm
∠B=70°AC=4cm	∠E=55° DF=3.2cm	∠H=20° GI=2cm
∠C=55°AB=3.5cm	∠F=90° DE=4cm	∠I=45°GH=3.7cm

a.	△ABC	△DEF	△GHI
	∠B	∠F	∠G
	AC	DE	HI

b. Yes, in all the three triangles

c.	△ABC	△DEF	△GHI
	∠A&∠C	∠D	∠H
	BC&AB	EF	GI

d. Yes, in all the three triangles

Revision Exercise

1.   **a.**   1,30,445,   1,30,645,   1,30,845
     b.   1,46,080,   1,76,080,   1,86,080

2.   **a.**   4,73,199   **b.**   44,711
     c.   111.08

3.   **a.** $\frac{2}{18}$ $\frac{3}{27}$ $\frac{4}{36}$
     b. $\frac{6}{8}$ $\frac{9}{12}$ $\frac{12}{16}$
     c. $\frac{4}{10}$ $\frac{6}{15}$ $\frac{8}{20}$
     d. $\frac{10}{12}$ $\frac{15}{18}$ $\frac{20}{24}$

4.   **a.**   28   **b.**   7   **c.**   90

5.   **a.**   7.5 cm each
     b.   12 days

6.   **a.**   0.2   **b.**   0.4
     c.   0.5   **d.**   0.6

7.   0.45,   0.54,   4.05,   5.04

8.   **a.**   20,40,60,80
     b.   H.C.F.=6,   L.C.M.=72

9.   Rs 97   **10.**   87 $\frac{5}{8}$ kg

11.   5.73 m each

12.   **a.**   4.8   **b.**   386
     c.   0.1   **d.**   0.012

13.   **a.** $\frac{4}{16}$ **b.** $\frac{2}{8}$ **c.** $\frac{6}{8}$

14.   **a.**   5   **b.**   50
     c.   10.9   **d.**   10.7

15.   **a.**   750.4   **b.**   8.9
     c.   1479   **d.**   706

16.   **a.**   9   7   3   6
     b.   10   100
     c.   10   100
     d.   9 hundredths

18.   28 pupils

19.   **a.**   5 $\frac{3}{5}$ **b.**   13 $\frac{6}{7}$
     c.   3 $\frac{7}{8}$ **d.**   15 $\frac{1}{5}$

20.   1.714 bars of chocolate (approx.)

21.   **a.**   15   **b.**   20   **c.**   72

22.   Rs 6402

23.   **a.**   32078   **b.**   57876
     c.   33 $\frac{1}{24}$ **d.**   45 $\frac{11}{14}$

24.   **a.** $\frac{12}{15}$ $\frac{16}{20}$ $\frac{20}{25}$

     b. $\frac{27}{23}$ $\frac{81}{189}$ $\frac{243}{567}$

25.   9.74

26.   Each part has a right angle *(read kind of angle has each part? after what)*

27.   **a.**   7 kg 160 gm
     b.   1 kg 300 gm
     c.   2 hr 52 min
     d.   2 hr 39 min *(read mm as min)*

28.   **a.**   9 $\frac{1}{3}$,   9 $\frac{1}{3}$ **b.**   4 $\frac{1}{6}$
     c.   2 $\frac{1}{8}$ **d.**   2 $\frac{5}{6}$

29.   **a.**   3000 tickets
     b.   4032 glasses

30.   **a.** $\frac{2}{3}$ **b.** $\frac{1}{12}$ **c.**   12 $\frac{5}{6}$ m

31.   9 m

32.   **a.**   3832   **b.**   2676

33.   0.04, 0.046, 0.4, 0.46, 0.64, 1.6

34.   **a.**   17.4   **b.**   38.75
     c.   45.6   **d.**   78.5

35.   13.72 kg

36.   Rs 26,   Rs 39

37.   **a.**   **b.**

38.   8,367

39.   3,81,046

40.   **a.**   2,83,499   **b.**   11,210

41.   16 oranges each

42.   **a.** $\frac{9}{16}$ **b.**   2 $\frac{5}{8}$

43.   **a.**   25 $\frac{2}{3}$
     b.   49, 35, 28, 14

44.   6   7   2

45.   2,4

46.   8

47.   **a.** $\frac{2}{5}$ **b.** $\frac{21}{10}$
     c. $\frac{51}{5}$ **d.** $\frac{263}{10}$

48.   8

49.   216 people

50. 6 parts

51. 54 m

52. Rs 617.70

53. **a.** 9535 **b.** 9.422
c. 8049.60

54. **a.** 81 **b.** 56
c. 11 **d.** 10

55. **a.** more than the denominator
b. less than the denominator
c. whole number and a fraction

56.

Common fractions	$\frac{72}{100}$	$\frac{61}{1000}$	$\frac{3}{4}$	$\frac{8803}{1000}$	$9\frac{2}{5}$	$\frac{103}{10}$	$\frac{912}{100}$	$\frac{7}{20}$
Decimal fractions	0.72	0.061	0.75	8.803	9.4	10.3	9.12	0.35

57. **a.** 1.4 **b.** 0.8 **c.** 1.9
d. 1.4 **e.** 1.52 **f.** 8.52

58. **a.** 9 **b.** 20.6 **c.** 86
d. 5.8 **e.** 0.06 **f.** 0.008
g. 0.13 **h.** 0.0478

59. 8, 16, 24, 32, 40, 48, 56, 64, 72, 80
16, 32, 48, 64, 80, 96, 112, 128, 144, 160
Common multiples —
16, 32, 48, 64, 80
LCM = 16

60. **a.** $1101\frac{1}{8}$ gm **b.** $599\frac{5}{8}$ gm

61. **a.** $16\frac{6}{7}$ **b.** $135\frac{4}{7}$
c. $3\frac{15}{19}$ **d.** Re 0.25

62. **a.** 1,13,576 **b.** 2,14,107
c. 5,56,560 **d.** 3,27,754

63. **a.** 2,325 **b.** 15,380

64. $3\frac{1}{6}$ apples **65.** $\frac{221}{28}$

66. 55 rubber bands

67. 23,40,406

68. 2,65,340

69. **a.** 12,21,179 **b.** 2,78,774

70. **a.** 2 **b.** 3.5 **c.** 1.8
d. $5\frac{1}{3}$ **e.** 5 **f.** 13
g. $9\frac{3}{4}$ **h.** $6\frac{7}{8}$

71. 12 boxes

72. **a.** town C 24,232
town A 52,354
town B 61,058
town D 91,508

b. 2,29,152

73. $7\frac{7}{80}$ cm

74. 2038 men; 1019 women

75. **a.** 6.125 m
b. 1.416 kg

76. 62213 letters

77. 1.5%

78. 13640.4

79. Each child gets $\frac{1}{8}$ of an orange.

80. **a.** Wednesday
b. Monday
c. Rs 480

81. **a.** 3hr 44min
b. 2 weeks 4 days
c. 6 years 8 months

82. **a.** 4843 gm
b. 2458 m

83. **a.** 55 minutes
b. 25.5 lit

84. **a.** 6 cm, 3 cm
b. 18 cm

85. $60\frac{2}{3}$ lit

86. 6.7 kg

87. 2610 lit

88. 12

89. 35 days

90. 460 sec